Greetings, Dover!

from
Jack Hewitt

Compiled and edited by Derek Leach

Riverdale Publications
24 Riverdale River Dover Kent CT17 0QX

This book is dedicated to
all my friends both past and present

Published in 2002 by D A Leach (Riverdale Publications)
24 Riverdale, River, Dover, Kent CT17 0QX

ISBN 0 9536166 3 0

Printed in England by A R Adams & Sons (Printers) Ltd.
The Printing House, Dour Street, Dover, Kent CT16 1EW

CONTENTS

INTRODUCTION

Greetings, Dover! is the third in my trilogy of books about living local characters who have an interesting story to tell. Like Lillian Kay and Joe Harman, Jack Hewitt MBE is also unique in his own way. Like them, he is a Dovorian and very proud of it.

What sort of story does Jack have to share with us? Now a very active 90 years old, his memories of Dover go back to the First World War and, despite living in the same town as Lillian and Joe, he has quite different memories. He has given a lifetime of service to his fellow man, mainly, but not only, through his very many years in the scout movement and in the Order of St John. In both organisations he held and holds high office locally and was held in high esteem nationally. His 29 years in the County Ambulance Service also enabled Jack to serve through his paid work, which he loved and for which he was commended several times.

Jack has also travelled widely all over the world, both as a courier for many years for Raymond Cook Tours and as a seeker of unusual experiences in far flung parts of the world. Many of these holidays have enabled him to see members of St John in action in other countries. Seeking new experiences has been a lifelong aim, whether flying across the Channel as a young man or taking a hot air balloon ride on his 80th birthday!

His story is packed with amusing anecdotes, some of which are hard to believe, but Jack assures me that they are true. He is a cheeky chappy and has often 'got away with murder,' particularly during his war service, in order to have his way or to do what he thought was right. This cheeky chappy is also a cheerful chappy. He is often about town even now giving a cheerful word to everyone he meets, always beginning, of course, with 'Greetings!' Needless to say, anybody who has met Jack cannot forget his laugh. That is unique!

Derek Leach

Chapter 1

BORN AND 'BREAD'

Greetings! I was the third child of six in my family with two brothers and three sisters. Mother had a child every two years except for Jean who came seven years later. Every two years my father would have a photograph taken of the whole family, which I didn't think much of then but it is very nice to look back upon now. I was born in Crafford Street, Dover on 13 February 1912. Father, a Dovorian, was called James. He was born in1883 and died aged 64 in 1947. Grandfather Hewitt was a carpenter from Ramsgate and he married a local girl whose surname was Smithers. Grandfather Brown helped to build the extension to the Admiralty Pier working in a diving bell. When he was young he swept the chimney of the Chartham Asylum. Mother, Mary Brown, came from Chartham. I don't know how Mum and Dad met

We had a house and bakery. The shop and the front bedroom were in Crafford Street and the rest of the house and the bakery were in Dour Street. The beautiful tree, which now stands where the bake house stood, is a *Caucasias wingnut*, a native of Iran. Hewitt Road that is there now was named after the family in 1980. Father was a master baker and he opened the business when he was 16. It wasn't

Gran and Grandpa Hewitt

Gran and Grandpa Brown

Mum and Dad's wedding photograph, 1906

until 1938 that he finished paying off the loan from Mannering, the miller, which he had to have to start the business, so we never had any spare money. We were comfortable. We never had holidays but we always had enough good food. My parents were good and kind and we were happy. We were satisfied with what we had in those days and didn't worry about what other people had. Then World War II came along and the whole lot went.

The roof of the bake house collapsed in 1944 when it was hit by the next to last shell to fall on Dover. It was raining heavily and my father heard a few tiles falling then the whole roof caved in. Fortunately, the loft floor prevented the debris from damaging the bake house itself. My father, who was in the

A family photograph taken when Jack was about 13.
From the left: Leonard, Mother, Leslie, little sister Jean, Father, Jack, Eileen and Bertha

Hewitt's Bakery after shell damage

Crafford Street following shell damage, 13 September 1944

kitchen, thought that an aircraft had crashed on to the house. The crash was heard by a great many people and soon there was a crowd outside. Despite all the rubble that fell into the road, nobody was injured.

Earliest memories

Apparently when I was three I had lovely curly hair, but soon after I had my photograph taken, I rubbed shoe blacking in it one day and had to have it all cut off. My earliest memory was during the First World War. My brother and I were sent to Goodnestone (pronounced Gunstone) to live. I stayed with my auntie at the end of Goodnestone Park and my

Site of the Hewitt bakery

Jack aged 3

Leslie, Eileen and Jack (right) aged 4

brother stayed in a farmhouse opposite. I was 4 years old and went to Goodnestone School. One day the teacher said, 'You've got quite a good voice and we've got the Honourable Mr Plumptre coming down and I would like you to sing.' So I had to learn this song, *My Daddy's gone to be a soldier*, which I know to this very day. I had to walk through Goodnestone Park to get to school and opposite the mansion was a tree with a seat all the way round it, which was a favourite of mine because its bark was nice and soft. Later, when I knew more about trees, I discovered that it was a Californian Redwood (*sequoia gigantum*); it was still there the last time I went, a few years ago.

On one occasion I came back home from Goodnestone for a weekend and was in the kitchen on my own when I heard this terrific bang. I shouted and my father came in and asked what was wrong. Then a policeman put his head through the window and asked if we were all right! It was a shell going over the town fired from a submarine outside the harbour. When I came back home to live I went to a little private school in Dour Street, at number 59, run by Miss Hoult. There were 20 of us and I stayed until I was about eight. She taught all of us in one room with two to a desk and there was one outside toilet. It was quite packed. Our playground was the house's back garden. Her mother lived with her in the house.

St Mary's School

From Miss Hoult's I went to St Mary's Boys' School in Queen Street. It was a good school. It had a school song, *Success to all St Mary's Boys*, which nobody knows these days. The Old Boys' Association has wound up and we only have St Mary's Primary School now. They were good days.

St Mary's School, Queen Street

5

St Mary's School, prior to demolition

You could possibly say that the history of the school began in 1616 when Robert Udney was asked by the Corporation to run a school for six poor children for a salary of £8 per annum in part of the old St Martin le Grand buildings, which had been used as a Court Hall.

The present St Mary's Primary School claims its birth from the founding, in 1789, of the Charity School for 40 boys and 20 girls in Queen Street on the site of the present museum. To make a living wage for the master and mistress the school had to be enlarged to take 65 boys and 45 girls.

In 1820 private subscriptions allowed a new school to be built, again in Queen Street, open to all poor children, with living accommodation for the two teachers. Apparently, 200 boys and 200 girls were taught in two rooms.

The 1870 Education Act made elementary education compulsory for all children and in 1871 the school became a trust under the umbrella of the National Education Society. In the 1820 premises the boys were taught in the lower room with girls in the upper room, but from 1872 a new building on the corner of Queen Street and Princes Street catered for the girls and an infants' school, leaving the old premises for the boys. The School Committee, chaired by Canon Puckle, Vicar of St Mary's, managed the schools with the curate acting as secretary and collecting the 'school pence' every week. They had a hectic time getting the old and new buildings into shape, acquiring desks etc and solving the noise problem in the old building by filling in the space between the floor joists with sawdust!

St Mary's Schools were evacuated to Wales during the Second World War; 152 boys plus staff went. The schools reopened in 1945. In 1949 all children over 11 years were transferred to secondary modern or grammar schools in the town and St Mary's boys' and girls' schools were amalgamated to form St Mary's Church of England Mixed Primary School and the separate infants' school was amalgamated in 1960. By then pupils numbered almost 400 with a head and 13 teachers.

The school eventually fell victim to the construction of the York Street dual carriageway and was demolished, revealing that it had been sitting on the headquarters of the Roman fleet! The present school, off Maison Dieu Road, was built and opened in 1969.

Head teachers were required to keep a school log and to make an entry, no matter how short, every day. Amongst all the details of teachers' absences and of visitors, such as the school attendance officer, school dentist, school nurse, Diocesan inspectors, religious instruction inspectors and HMI inspectors, other information gives a good picture of life there and makes interesting reading. These logs are now in the Canterbury Cathedral archives.

When the boys' school opened in 1871 there were 79 boys with one master, Mr Howells, assisted by three pupil teachers (trainees). Pupil numbers soon rose to 120. By 1902 there were 16 teachers assisting Mr Howells. During the First World War there were all sorts of problems caused by lighting restrictions, air raids, shortages of teachers, pupils being sent to the country at night for safety and, in 1918, the influenza epidemic forced the school to close, first for two weeks and then for three. On Armistice Day there was such celebrating in the town that only a quarter of children attended and so the school closed for the day, followed quickly by a week's holiday!

The log book entries often complain about poor attendance caused by bad weather, illness and, in September, by hop-picking.

In 1919, when school fees were abolished, there were 505 boys on the books with three classes in the lower room and another three in the upper one. All the local peace treats and the main Dover Peace Treat interfered with lessons in that year. Many old boys had been killed and the Old Boys' Association provided a war memorial tablet at the school, which was unveiled in 1920. More time was lost with a day's holiday for Sir William Crundall's treat for Dover's children and another day for the unveiling of the Dover Patrol memorial. We seemed to have quite a few extra holidays of one sort or another. The school always closed for

A class at St Mary's School

7

Sunday School treats – in 1920 for six successive Wednesday afternoons! If St Mary's Church fete and the Regatta were held in term time, the school closed. The king's birthday was another holiday when there was a military parade. On Ascension Day we would have a service at St Mary's Church with the rest of the day off. Major Astor, the Dover MP and Lady Violet Astor always paid for the school's Christmas treat – in 1926 we went to the Queen's Hall for some films, followed by tea at school and presents of oranges and sweets.

By 1922, when I was at the school, the numbers were limited to 488 boys. Mr Wicks was the headmaster with 10 teachers. He retired in 1923 after 51 years at the school as pupil, pupil teacher and then, after college, assistant master in 1883 and headmaster from 1909 when Mr Howells retired. Mr Wellden, a teacher at the school from 1900 became Head (and did not retire until 1945 after 46 years at the school).

The school's inspection report in 1924 tells us that running the school wasn't easy. There were 450 boys of great diversity and problems with premises. Whilst there was a room for each class the playground was very small, only 130 square yards; playtime had to be in two shifts. A new playground was opened later the same year for physical education. Teaching was said to be diligent and efficient with many of the boys coming from homes where the value of education was appreciated. Quality of work in the upper school was good. Arithmetic and elementary maths were well taught; handwriting was good with compositions 'reasonably free from blunders'. Surprisingly, French was taught to all boys in the top three classes but the inspector thought classes were too large for this subject and bearing in mind no homework was done little progress could be expected. The school soon took the hint and dropped French. In the lower school there were a large number of 'backward' boys with 40 over 11 years who had been in these classes for several years. The inspector recognised the problem but stated that these boys should not stay in classes with much younger lads. In those days you 'went up' on ability not age; nevertheless, some of these youngsters were soon promoted. He commented on the boys' enthusiasm and success at sports with 80 able to swim and also noted the flourishing Old Boys' Association.

I wasn't exceptionally good at anything really, but I liked geography. I wasn't very good at spelling unfortunately. I had a stutter then and I was threatened with the cane to try to stop it but I think it only made it worse. You had to go to the Headmaster for the cane. I got it once when I was 13. Our teacher, Mr Woods, was leaving to be a teacher at a Borstal (Institution) and I went to the front of the class and said that Mr Woods had been jolly good to us and we should give him a leaving present. So I collected the money and two or three of us decided to get him a box of cigarettes from Williams' the tobacconists at the bottom of the street. Anyway, Mr Woods spotted me in front of the class and asked me what I was doing. I said, 'Nothing much.' 'You must have been doing something,' he said angrily. So I said, 'It was just something I said to the boys that I can't repeat to you.' He said, 'If you don't tell me, you'll get the stick,' which I did – four strokes. Of course, when I made the presentation later on he realised what he had done.

We had a small playground, which was packed at playtime with about 200 boys at a time. There were no facilities for sport although it was a great school for swimming. We went to the saltwater baths on the sea front for three quarters of an hour every week. The annual school sports were held at Crabble Athletic Ground. In addition to the usual races, long jump, high jump etc, there were blindfold races, three-legged races, sack races, egg and spoon races and obstacle races. Because of my illness as a boy I couldn't do sports, but I did enter the three-legged and egg and spoon races as well as the fancy dress competition.

On the day my Uncle Fred was getting married I was told to wear my best suit to school, which I only wore on Sundays normally. Mother told me not to come straight home but to take a walk on the sea front and come home at about 5 o'clock. Where Pencester Gardens are now used to be a tan yard and there was a tree right across the river. I decided to climb this tree and cross the river but I fell in! I was in trouble!

General elections were great times during my school life. Major Astor was the Conservative MP for many years and, on one occasion, he was opposed by Sir Thomas Polson, an anti-waste candidate. Major Astor used to give away rabbits to the poor at Christmas. We boys had fun chanting:

> *'Vote, vote, vote for Major Astor,*
> *Kick old Polson out the door,*
> *If it wasn't for the law,*
> *We'd break his bloomin' jaw*
> *And we won't vote for Polson anymore.'*

Sometimes this would cause fights in the school playground, but masters always stepped in before they got out of hand. Another great time, which has disappeared now, was Empire Day. There would be a big Union Jack in the playground and the whole school would sing Rule Britannia and God Save the King followed by a half day holiday. Another custom, which was rather strange, was when the Oxford and Cambridge Boat Race was held. All the children would support Oxford or Cambridge and wear light or dark blue colours. I always supported Cambridge. Years later, my cousin, Percy Erith, who lived in Folkestone, rowed for Cambridge.

There was a hairdresser in Woolcomber Street, called Lamiday, and I went after school one day for a haircut, but he had a lot of comics and I let everybody else go in front of me so that I could go on reading the comics. It got late and nobody at home knew where I was; they had forgotten that I was going to the barber's. My father called the police to help search for me. I wasn't too popular!

In the soup

During my school days my brothers and I used to take bread, 4lb sandwich loaves, down to the Council's soup kitchen in Ladywell underneath the Connaught Hall. One day I delivered the bread and when I got home Dad asked me where I had been as I had been gone more than an hour. So I said that I had had soup in the kitchen. Dad made me go back and apologise because the soup was for the very poor and we weren't that poor! There was a big demand for the soup kitchen in those days with so many out of work.

I missed quite a lot of schooling due to illness and so, after I left school, I started evening classes at Ladywell, studying commercial arithmetic and business economics. My teacher was Miss Rookwood who also taught at Dover County School. 'Good evening, Hewitt,' she said and I replied, 'Good evening, Rookwood!' I told my father and he made me apologise. Looking back now I think that I must be dyslexic, because I often 'read' extra words that are not in fact printed – even when I sing hymns!

Snargate Street in its heyday

Pastimes

There was a wonderful toy-shop in Snargate Street called Pointers that sold boxes of soldiers. We would have a box for Christmas and then a fort the next Christmas, adding a couple of soldiers when we could. Most of the time we played outside with hoops, tops, conkers and

Part of Ladywell prior to demolition in 1930s

Ladywell//Dour Street corner with site clearance for police station pre WW2

hoop-la. It doesn't sound much compared with the toys of today but they gave us a lot of pleasure.

Travelling fairs were always popular when they came to Dover. I remember especially a joywheel that was like a big record that sloped down from the centre and you had to get on it. My brother and I became experts. We used to win prizes and get free rides. There was always a boxing booth where the boxers would challenge any man to have a go at them. That was really exciting to watch.

Robin Hood

One of the games we used to play was Robin Hood and I was usually Robin Hood. We used to make good bows from ash sticks and play in 'Monkey's Island' at the top of Connaught Park. On a very windy day I told my younger brother that I had a good idea: to jump off the bank using Mum's umbrella as a parachute. I did it. The umbrella turned inside out; I badly grazed my knees and was in trouble when I got home! We played games like 'Jack, Jack, show a light' and, naughtily, we tied people's doorknockers together. Apart from that we hired cycles from Niblett's in Park Street at 6d per hour. There was Binfield's the grocers on the corner and then Niblett's with a shed full of bikes. We cycled round and round the block: Park Street, Maison Dieu Road, Crafford Street and Dour Street. Of course, there wasn't much traffic about then. When the time was up we would have a quick ride up Albert Road, down Frith Road and back to Niblett's where we would be told off for being ten minutes late, but he never charged us extra!

I used to go swimming in the harbour sometimes but it was never a great love because as soon as I got into cold water it would take my breath away. My brothers and sisters used to go. In those days so many people went to the beach that you had to spread a mackintosh out on the ground to save your pitch. If you were caught undressing on the beach, you were fined. Policemen were always on the watch for you. You had to use the changing huts unless it was early in the morning. I remember seeing a neighbour of ours, Mrs Lott, coming out of a changing hut in long stockings dressed up as though she was going shopping rather than for a swim!

Facts of life

At the age of nine when my mother was going to have another baby, I was very naive and didn't have a clue about the facts of life. I wasn't naughty, but I was mischievous. When the baby was due I was sent off to Nonington to stay with Mr and Mrs Cassidy. He was a foreman miner. I had never met them before but I was quite happy there. I kept asking when this baby was coming and was told it was on its way from Scotland. I asked every day and said that it must be a very slow train. Then I asked whether it was going to be a boy or a girl and was told they couldn't tell because it was all wrapped up! I can't imagine children of nine today being fooled like that. I eventually heard about the facts of life from playground talk. There was certainly no sex education in school and nothing from my parents. There was no experimentation and no pressure upon us to find out, unlike today. Up to about the same age we all believed in Father Christmas. I think children miss out these days with real childhood being so short.

While I was at Nonington I kept pestering Mr Cassidy to go down the Snowdown coal mine and eventually managed it. Snowdown was the deepest of the four mines in Kent. Going down the pit shaft was like bungee jumping – you dropped like a stone for a mile! That is like dropping down about 17 Shakespeare Cliffs at once! This was in 1923, I think, when there were still pit ponies and I took down sugar lumps for them. In later years, after the Second World War, I visited all the other Kent mines taking parties of senior scouts and ambulance personnel. I never let on that I had been down before and always said that it was a great privilege and a wonderful experience, which it was.

Singing in the workhouse

On several occasions when I was about 12, I went with my uncle up Union Road (now Coombe Valley Road) to the Union Workhouse or Poor Law Institution, which is now Buckland Hospital. On the way we passed a hose reel and ambulance station. There were a number of these located around the town housing a stretcher on wheels, Furley litters they were called after their inventor Sir John Furley. Where the hospital car park is now used to be like allotments where down and outs passing through Dover needing a place to stay would have to work for their bed. Many of Dover's very poor lived in the workhouse all the time, but had to do the washing and cleaning etc,. You didn't get something for nothing in those days and I think that was a good principle if you were fit enough. The Master of the Union was Mr Godden and the Matron, Mrs Plews. Once my uncle and I went to entertain the inmates. He had a lovely tenor voice and always sang *When you're a happy friend of mine*. Another thing that went down well was when he sat in an armchair on the stage with his face black, a miner's lamp by his feet and with me sitting on a stool looking up at him singing *Don't go down the mine, Daddy, things very often come true*. When I was in India during the Second World War, I visited my uncle and went to the Anglo-Indian Club where he sang his familiar song.

Shops

Sometimes my mother used to call me John Willy and then I knew I had to do an errand for her. One shop I liked to go to was the Maypole where I knew all the staff. Lots of things were sold loose. The butter would be patted, the cheese cut and a big scoop would weigh out stuff from sacks: sultanas, raisins etc. Everybody in the shops was so friendly. There was a grocer's shop at the bottom of our street called Binfield's – the proprietor had a face as white as chalk. We used to go there to get broken biscuits because they were cheap. On one occasion, when I was about ten, I asked for broken biscuits but he said that he didn't have any. So I kicked a box over and said, 'You have now!' I told my parents and they made me go back to apologise and my father paid for the box of broken biscuits!

I very much enjoyed walking past Cave's Café in Bench Street and taking in that beautiful smell of coffee. I never went in as a boy, but I did later when the manager was Mr Bodensiech.

Cinemas and theatres

There were five cinemas in Dover when I was young. I went to the Wellington in Snargate Street mostly and sometimes the Queen's Hall in Queen Street. The films were silent but there was a lady pianist who played wonderful, suitable music to accompany them. We used to cheer, especially when Tom Mix came on; he was my favourite with his horse, Tony. There was often a serial with Pearl White being tied on a railway line and the train approaching. We brothers went in the afternoon for about 3d each.

We didn't go to the Hippodrome Theatre in Snargate Street as children because of the price. Even

Queen's Hall, Queen Street

13

Queen's Hall during demolition in the 1970s

though we were in business we were quite poor. There were six of us to feed and doctors' bills to pay when we were ill. We used to bath on Saturday nights in this great big galvanised bath, which was put on the big kitchen table. When we were older we went on Sunday mornings to the public baths, now the Biggin Hall. My younger brother and I shared a bath – two for the price of one.

No outings or holidays

We couldn't go to places like some children. I remember a school outing to a London exhibition that a couple of my friends were going to, but my mother said that their father was an engine driver and could afford it; she couldn't. (I didn't go to London until I was 20. When I was called up during the War and had to report to Gloucester, I thought I was going halfway round the world on that train journey.) There was no money for family outings. We didn't get any pocket money, but sometimes we would be given a 1d to take a tram somewhere for an errand, but we would run there instead and spend the penny on sweets. You could get quite a lot for a penny. A Saturday treat that we all looked forward to was Dad bringing home from Mrs Sibley's shop in Snargate Street a threepenny Dover bag for each of us containing pieces of sweet rock, bulls' eyes and other sweets plus a small toy.

The Merrymakers

When I was about 12 years old I formed the Merrymakers Club, which met in our front room. My parents went to the Royal Hippodrome in Snargate Street every Monday evening. That was their special pleasure. I said to my brothers and sisters that Monday evenings would be a good time to form a club that could meet at our house. The members were the five Hewitts, the two Rouse brothers, Edith and George Barton, Chalky White, Bobby Edmonds and Willy Doble. Subscriptions were a 1d or 2d. One member would buy cakes from our shop at 2 for a penny and another would bring the lemonade powder. We made our own enjoyment. My oldest sister Eileen was 16 then and she played the piano. Our favourite song was When it's springtime in the Rockies. The rest of the time would be spent playing darts, draughts, ludo, snakes and ladders, dominoes etc. Only one neighbour, Mrs Lott, complained about the noise and my mother would say that we were not doing any harm. The place was always clean and tidy when my parents came home. Then one Monday evening my parents came home early because Mum was feeling unwell and that was the end of the club, because they didn't know anything about it. It lasted a long time. The little money that we had accumulated went to the Royal Victoria Hospital.

Royal Hippodrome, Snargate Street

Boy Scout

I joined the Charlton Church Choir when I was 12 and stayed until I was 16. I was also a server. I also joined the 23rd Dover Sea Scouts. The Scoutmaster was Mr Curtis and he was a missionary to seamen at the Northampton Street Bethel.

The only holiday I had before the War was with the Sea Scouts. It was a camp at Beltinge. We had a race from Beltinge to Reculver – miles and miles, it seemed to me. I didn't quite come in last. There was an apple orchard at the bottom of our field and I wandered down there with another scout. There were hundreds of apples. I said, 'The farmer won't miss a few. We'll take back enough for two for everybody in our tent, twelve in total.' My friend said that it was

Jack, aged 13, Charlton Church Choir

Jack with brother Leslie in the Sea Scouts and sister Eileen in the Girl Guides, 1924

stealing, but I disagreed. There were so many there that nobody would miss them! The farmer spotted us and we made a quick getaway. The next morning we saw the scoutmaster talking to the farmer. Then the scoutmaster called out that two scouts had been seen in the orchard stealing apples and asked for the two boys to come out. Well, scouts are honest, so we went out. The farmer was so pleased with our honesty that he supplied us with rhubarb for three days, but we didn't get any apples! That was the first and last time I stole anything.

As my good turn, every Friday night I used to clean the cannons outside the Library. I was in the Sea Scouts for only about six months because I was always seasick so I left and joined the Charlton Scouts – they had a brass band. I stayed and became Assistant Scout-master and then I started my own troop on the Western Heights, the 6th Dover Westcliff Military Troop. The Highland Light Infantry was stationed there at the time. Captain Bailey Stewart bought us a tent – later, he was imprisoned as a spy during the War! I was going to St Margaret's Bay with some Charlton Scouts and some kiddies came up to me and said, 'We'd like to be in the Scouts.' So I asked where they came from and they were soldiers' sons from the Western Heights. I said that I would see what I could do. So I went

and talked to the padre at the Western Heights. He offered to give me a lift up if I started a troop up there, so I did. Unfortunately, he didn't take me home so I used to go home down the Grand Shaft and round that way. That was when I was about 25. With war threatening the military closed the troop in 1938 and put the area out of bounds.

Delivery boy

At 14 I left school and did baking in our bakery, but I never liked it. I did the deliveries to the homes of our regular customers most of the day with a barrow or a bike. I went out at about 8am, came home for lunch and then went out again, returning at 5 or 6 o'clock. On Saturdays it was later. One of the jobs I did before I left school was to cycle with the bread up to the Coastguard Cottages on the cliffs, either at dinner time or more usually after tea. There

Jack, aged 16

Coastguard houses, East Cliff

were eight houses up there at the top of the cliff path; Hewitt's delivered to five of them. You weren't allowed to ride down the path. I was caught once and warned. One day I saw a policeman in the shop at the bottom. I thought that he would probably wait to catch me riding back down. So I pushed my bike right over Northfall Meadow and came down Waterworks Hill. Two or three days later I saw him and he asked what had happened to me – I had gone up the path but had not come back. So I said that I knew he would be waiting for me and I had gone over Northfall Meadow!

There were 37 bakers in Dover and 32 of them delivered. Sometimes you would see three bakers' barrows in the same street. A man used to go round the streets selling winkles for tea on Sundays and another man, a basket maker from Northampton Street, called Grognet, would go round the streets calling, 'Rasket, tasket, chair or basket.' Rag and bone men would give you a goldfish in a jam jar in exchange for some rags.

Horses

In my young days most of the tradesmen used horse drawn vehicles for deliveries. There were plenty of them about: bakers' vans, millers' wagons, brewers' drays, coal merchants' wagons, hearses and Sir William Crundall's carriage!

Monkey business

When I was about 20 I was walking along the sea front one summer evening when I met Captain Bellchamber whom I used to serve with bread. Much to my surprise, he was carrying a monkey. He told me that he had been recalled to his regiment and had to get rid of his pet. He lived in Priory Grove. I said that I would buy it and did so. I took it home and it climbed on to the dresser. Father came into the kitchen and the monkey jumped onto his shoulder. Father screamed, 'You and the monkey get out. Stay out until you get rid of that monkey!' I was still out at 9 o'clock wondering what to do. Then I thought of Edward Mannering, the miller, who lived at River in the Old Vicarage and had a fox cub and goats etc. So I rang him up and told him the story. He offered to come and collect it in the morning, but I said it would have to be now! He came and took it off me and I went home!

Customs cake

One day, I received a call from the Customs Office, which was at 29 Waterloo Crescent then, telling me that a packet had arrived for me and asking for permission to open it. I refused, but said that I would go down to their office. It was a large piece of wedding cake, black in colour, which they probed until they were satisfied. None of the family would eat any of this jolly cake, so I had it all to myself. It was good with rum, cherries and spices in it – the best cake I've ever tasted. It came from a friend of mine in Jamaica, Percy Walcott. Although we had corresponded for years, I never heard from him again after the wedding. There were bad floods out there and I think he must have been drowned.

Jack delivering bread, aged 22

My goodness, my Guinness

I was secretary of the local blood transfusion service for four years until the outbreak of war in 1939. At that time it was a 'silent service,' which few people knew about. I had to keep a list of names and addresses of all donors, only about 20 of them, who could be called on to give blood. In those days donated blood couldn't be stored. When some was needed the hospital would contact the police and they would contact me. At first, it was mainly policemen who gave blood. Later, members of the public gave blood, too. If one fainted, several more would faint. When I gave blood I asked Dr Erskine and Dr Piper for my Guinness, but they laughed. I insisted that I was entitled to a Guinness. 'No, you're not.' 'Yes, I am.' They took me upstairs and gave me one. They had plenty! After that they always offered me a Guinness during my years as blood donor secretary and any donors that wanted one.

On one occasion, I had just finished my baker's round at the back of St Mary's Church at about 8pm when a policeman found me and said I was needed to give blood for an emergency. Doctor Cobbe took two pints and said that I was fit and would be all right; but I wasn't! My father was annoyed and so was my brother – he had to go and collect my baker's barrow!

Chapter 2

SECOND WORLD WAR

Dover ARP

I stayed with the bakery firm until the beginning of the War. Father wondered what would become of the business and I said that all the people from Dover would leave and bread wouldn't be needed. I stayed for a year and became an Air Raid Precaution (ARP) first aid team leader at the Ladywell First Aid Post. My training in the St John Ambulance Brigade stood me in good stead. I would be

Ladywell, 1940

delivering bread, then the siren would go and I would leave my barrow or bike, stop the first vehicle going in my direction, get into my overalls – I had always had my tin hat and respirator with me anyway – and wait for things to happen. I had to go back later to pick up my barrow! One day I was delivering bread when this lorry drew up and a man I didn't know spoke to me. It was Bert Ward that I knew later as an ambulance driver, he said, 'Can you spare me a second? I want you to come up the road

Ladywell First Aid Post, September 1940 with Fred Mottersham, Pat Lincoln and Jack.

War damaged Museum, Market Square

with me.' We went to this yard at the bottom of Priory Hill steps in Tower Hamlets, which was the mortuary. On the lorry Bert had a dead German sailor who had been picked up from the shore. We laid him out on the slab. Then I looked around at the other bodies and there was Councillor Walker on one side and my Uncle Fred on the other; I didn't even know he had been killed – by a delayed bomb in Folkestone Road. My uncle worked for the gas board and he went into the bomb crater to check the gas pipes when the bomb blew up. One day we went to the Market Square after it had been hit, including the Museum. There were bits of stuffed animals all over the square. I have told the Museum people that the lion's head they still have used to have a body until that day.

Three men were walking along a street when a bomb fell; the man in the middle, Mr Ellenor, got up and walked away, but the other two were killed outright. At a First Aid Post a splinter from a shell decapitated Victor Abbott. On one occasion a young man came up to me as bombs were dropping and asked where to go. I pointed out a basement in Camden Crescent where I thought he would be safe, but bombs fell there. I never knew his name but I always felt responsible for his death.

Another chap got the recognition for one of my rescues. It was 11 September 1940 and German bombers attacked the sea front area of Dover, dropping 26 bombs, which caused heavy damage and killed 16 people. In the ruins of Townwall Passage a young mother saved her five months old baby, Jean Amos, by throwing her body over the child. At the time it was reported that a Royal Navy stoker tunnelled his way under debris to rescue the baby. The story was told again in the *Dover Express* in 1980 and a Mrs Coleman said that she was that baby. So I told the newspaper that I had saved her. I was in charge of a four-man first aid party and I saw this stoker working further down the road with another rescue party. As we were about to leave, one of our group thought he heard a baby's cry. We all listened and heard it too, so I started tunnelling through the debris and after about 30 minutes I found the baby, but the mother was dead with her arms wrapped around it. It was the only time I cried throughout the War. It wasn't the fault of the stoker that he got the credit. In those days we were far too busy to worry about that sort of thing. I later learned that I was recommended for the George Medal, but apparently it was turned down because I should not have been doing rescue work as a first aid man! After that newspaper story I went and called on Mrs Coleman. It was a meeting full of memories.

In my scrapbook I have this poem written about Dover during the War:

Jack with Mrs Coleman, née Jean Amos, in 1980

The spirit of Dover 1943

Though bombs and shells come whizzing over,
Which test our courage here in Dover;
Though dwellings, buildings crash to earth
In this old town which gave us birth,
We carry on, though few in number,
Awakened often from our slumber;
Undaunted, valiant, bold and free
And thankful for our liberty.
Like gallant Malta, we'll hold on fast
Till our fears and dangers, too, have passed:
Praying to Him, all-wide and great,
At a crucial time – never late –
To comfort and help us safely through,
As He did at Mons and Dunkirk, too.
With thoughts like these, we're given heart
To carry on and play our part
Nobly and truly, from day to day,
Till final victory comes our way.
With pride, but humbly, I now ask,
As recognition of our task,
That soon, or when this war is over,
Some honour, too, be given – Dover .

Doctor Toland

When I was off duty I helped at Buckland Hospital where Doctor Gertrude Toland did a wonderful job throughout the Second World War. She gave 33 years as a consultant to the Dover hospitals, as a general practitioner in partnership with her husband and she also took an active part in the town's affairs. She was a governor of Dover's secondary schools from their inception, chairman of Dover

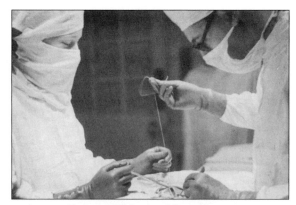

Dr GertrudeToland on left carrying out an emergency operation on a Dunkirk evacuee

County Youth Club and divisional surgeon of the Dover nursing division of the St John Ambulance Brigade. She was born in 1901 and came to Dover in 1932 when she married Patrick Toland who was already in practice in the town. She was the first woman to gain the higher qualification of Doctor of Medicine. Dr Toland stayed in Dover throughout the War. She spent long hours in the operating theatre dealing with the many victims of the shelling and bombing. Perhaps her greatest challenge was during the evacuation of Dunkirk when she worked tirelessly for nine days, operating on the severely injured troops landed at Dover. She and her husband both retired in 1968. She was widowed in 1979 and was made a Serving Sister of the Order of St John of Jerusalem before she died in 1990.

Royal Air Force

At the outbreak of the Second World War I volunteered for the Royal Air Force and went to the Canterbury Recruitment Centre. After the medical the major asked me which service I wanted to join and I said RAF. 'Well, you can't,' he said 'because the RAF Officer isn't here.' I replied, 'I'm a volunteer and if I can't go in the Air Force I won't go into anything!' The major said that I would be in trouble but I stood firm and came back home. I thought about it afterwards and decided to go and see a man I had done a good turn for years before, Air Commodore Leo Charlton, who lived at Victoria Park. He advised me to go straight back to Canterbury before I got into trouble. Luckily, I got there just before they closed and I saw this major who remembered me. 'What did you want to do in the RAF?' he said. 'Medical Orderly,' I replied. 'You can join the Royal Army Medical Corps,' he said. 'No, I can't. I want to go into the Air Force,' I replied. The Air Commodore had written a letter for me, which I showed to the major and he said that I was lucky because the RAF Officer was upstairs. He read the letter and said, 'All right, go home and you'll hear from us.' So I received my call-up papers, which told me to report to Gloucester on 26 December 1940 to be assessed for medical knowledge. When I turned up I was asked what I wanted. 'I've come to join the Air Force.' 'What! On Boxing Day?' was the reply. They didn't know what to do with me and four others who turned up with the same orders, so we slept on camp beds in the cloisters of Gloucester Cathedral. After two days assessment I was sent home until February 1941 when I started my square bashing at Blackpool. On the parade ground our Scottish flight sergeant used some very abusive language. I objected and was put on a charge but I managed to talk my way out of it!

Then I was posted to a hospital at Weeton where there were a lot of Polish patients. I got into more trouble when, after coming off night duty, I was ordered to go straight back on day duty to help nurse an officer with cerebral-spinal meningitis. I objected, because I wasn't trained to do it and was sent to Matron. She tore me off a strip and told me to get out!

I did my six weeks medical orderly training for the Princess Royal Nursing Service at RAF Halton. There was a flight sergeant lecturer there who used to take the rise out of me because of my laugh. He used to say, 'Everything's a piece of cake, everything's a piece of cake.' We weren't allowed to give gifts to the lecturers but I knew what I would do to get my own back. There was a lady in the village who used to give me a cup of tea when I passed through. So I asked her if she had any cake and she gave me a piece, which I wrapped in several layers of paper to look like a present. When the class was about to be dismissed, none of the others knew about it, I said, 'Flight Sergeant Hargreaves, I know that we're not supposed to do this, but on behalf of the class I've got a presentation to make to you.' The rest of the class looked at me wondering what was going on. I went to the front and gave him the parcel. He said that he shouldn't really accept it but as we had been such a good class he would. The class shouted at him to open it. I was sitting at the back when he did so. He was so mad that he chased me and I had to keep out of his way, but he couldn't put me on a charge or anything because he had accepted the present against all the rules!

Leonard Hewitt, RAMC, Jean Hewitt, RN and Jack, Princess Mary's Royal Nursing Service, RAF in 1941

Isle of Man

A flight sergeant asked me where I would like to be posted. I said that it didn't matter to me because if I said Dover, he would send me to Scotland. 'I'm sending you to Castletown. Do you know where that is?' I didn't. He said that it was in the Isle of Man. I went there but there was no RAF station there, I should have gone to Castletown in Scotland! So I went to the nearest RAF station, Ronaldsway airport, but they weren't expecting me either. I stayed there for a week doing nothing with my own room and a bed, then one of the chaps got posted and I took his place.

I was in the Isle of Man for exactly a year, based at the RAF gunnery school. While I was there, General de Gaulle came to speak at the opening of the Tynwald, the Manx Parliament. I said to the sergeant that I'd like to go and see it but he ummed and arred, so I went to the Medical Officer and asked him for the day off and he said that it was OK if it was all right with my sergeant. I went back to my sergeant and told him that the MO had given me permission, so I got my day off! De Gaulle towered over everybody else.

There was one thing that annoyed people on the Isle of Man and that was the Governor, Lord Granville. He was married to Queen Elizabeth's (now the Queen Mother) sister. When he went to the cinema in Douglas, usually with his wife and daughters, he always came in late. As soon as he arrived, the film was stopped, the lights went up and the National Anthem was played! On another occasion the governors of the children's home that I used to visit held an annual meeting and Lord Granville attended. I just happened to be there. The matron was invited in part way through the meeting and everybody stood up except for Lord Granville. He didn't stand apparently because he was the king's representative. I thought that was a bit arrogant.

All smiles in the Isle of Man

Wing Commander Jack

One day the Wing Commander poisoned his thumb and my sergeant was nervous about treating him, so he asked me to do it. When he came into the treatment room I had some lads waiting for treatment and so I asked them if they minded if I treated the Wing Commander first. Of course, I would have to anyway! Afterwards, he said, 'You've made a good job of that, and I may be able to return the compliment.' I immediately replied, 'Yes you can, sir. You can give me a flight around the island.' He agreed but weeks went by and I heard nothing about it even though I tried phoning him several times. I told my MO that I was determined to have that promised flight, so I went to the airport and spoke to the guard at the gate and said that when the Wing Commander passed through I wanted to stop him. 'You'll be put on a charge,' he said. Nevertheless, I put up my hand and said, 'Excuse me, sir, but you promised me a flight for treating your thumb and it's never materialised.' Within a week he phoned me and said that he would take me up to see a plane that had crashed on Scafell. I asked him to dip the plane when it passed over the Tower of Refuge and he asked jokingly whether I wanted to take over flying the plane as well! I crossed swords with him later. He used to come in and have a cup of tea with the MO nearly every day. The sick quarters used to get extra rations some of which I put into a stew for the lads, but I used the cheese to make cheese on toast for the Wing Commander and the MO to have with their tea. He came in one day and asked who took soup out to the gunnery site. The MO denied all knowledge, so did the sergeant even though they both knew. I said, 'I do, sir.' 'Do you get permission for this?' 'No, sir,' I replied. 'Where do you get the food from?' he wanted to know. 'From the food the men leave and the extra rations I make a stock pot that I keep going all the time and give it to the lads,' I said. 'It's got to stop,' he thundered. 'Fair enough, sir,' I answered. When he came in next day I made their tea and gave it to them. The Wing Commander asked why there was no cheese on toast, so I said, 'No soup for the lads on the gunnery site, no cheese on toast for the Wing Commander!' That went on for a fortnight and then he said that the soup could be resumed, so I gave them their cheese on toast.

Billy Ames

At one time the MO went on leave and the local doctor from the village was brought in. He wanted to know what to do if there were an accident. I said that there had only been one, but all he had to do was to follow me. No sooner had I said that than we had an accident! I had arranged a flying trip with a friendly pilot, Billy Ames, but he rang up and said that it

Billy Ames

27

was off because he had to take up a senior boy from King William College. Unfortunately, Billy's plane touched wings with another plane flown by Jackie Wells and had to make a forced landing. That was all right, but he went through a fence and both Billy and the boy were decapitated. I had to lay them out. I did it – with the help of another orderly – but it upset me so much that they gave me a week's leave. I should have been in that plane with Billy Ames.

On leave

Whilst on leave from the Isle of Man I was walking along Dover sea front when a shell landed on the saltwater baths. I was first on the scene. Some of the Green Howards were swimming there. The glass roof had shattered, many of the men were cut by flying glass and the blood turned the bathwater red; fortunately, only one man was badly cut.

Whilst I was on the Isle of Man, there was a Corporal Swann that I had to treat and he said, 'Jack, you've done a good job. I'll do something for you one day.' I immediately said, 'Well there is something you can do now. You've got that Triumph motor-bike and I'd like you take me round the T-T course!' He took me round at speed including one very steep hill. It was a terrific ride. So I can say that I've been round the Isle of Man T-T course.

Castletown Children's Home

Whilst I was on the island in my spare time I helped with the Castletown Scout Troop and at the Children's Home. One day I went into the shop in the village and a lady came in very upset. When she left I asked the shopkeeper who she was and apparently she was the matron of the children's home, which had been moved from Douglas to Castletown. Most of the staff had joined up and she didn't have enough helpers to cope with all the children. Later, I said to the Medical Officer, 'I've just had a telephone call from the Castletown Children's Home asking if I could help.' He said, 'Have they rung you, or have you rung them?' Anyway, I went to the home and found all these blitzed children from Liverpool with scabies. I took some stuff for it from the sick bay. The MO commented that we were using rather a lot of it and was I taking it to the children's home. I told him that quite a few of the gunnery trainees had rashes but he knew what I was up to! At Christmas the Speaker of the House of Keys came to the home, dressed up as Father Christmas and gave out presents to all the children. It was the most marvellous Christmas I ever had just seeing the faces of all those children.

Romance

During my time on the Isle of Man I grew very fond of a girl called Asenath Kelly, the only daughter of a draper in Douglas. I fell in love with her. She was a friend of the matron of the children's home that had moved from Douglas to Castletown. The week before I left for India, three naval officers were billeted on Asenath's parents. I told Asenath that it would be a long war and I could be away for three or four years. She would know these officers far better than she knew me and might fall in love with one of them. If so, so be it. Out in India I received a piece of wedding cake. She had married one of the naval captains. After the War he settled in the Isle of Man and became Head of Ramsey Grammar School. I only knew Asenath for three months but I still carry my one small photograph of her in my wallet.

I waited for some years, a long time after the War, but decided that, married or not, I must see her again. I found her father's house and he was still alive although in his sixties. I had only met him once before because I used to meet Asenath in the children's home. He said, 'Jack, you've come ten years too late. Asenath died of TB.' After that I didn't want anybody else. She was so nice. Perhaps that's why I put all my energies into voluntary work. It doesn't do to go back.

While I was there I went to the King William College and asked to

Asenath Kelly, 1941

see the Head. The bursar wanted to know why I wanted to see him. I told him that a friend of mine and a boy from the college had been killed in a flying accident during the War and I wondered whether there was a memorial to them at the school. 'Nobody was killed from this college,' he said. 'I beg your pardon,' I replied, 'but I was here during the War and I know they were killed.' He insisted that there was no memorial in the college and so did the Head who had been there five years. However, the lady in the office said that the village doctor during the War was dead but she knew his wife who remembered a medical orderly being very upset. The bursar phoned the widow and she told us to go into the school chapel and on the right hand side there was a brass memorial. I asked the Head to open the chapel and pointed to the memorial and said, 'I don't wish to be impertinent, sir, but there's the memorial that you know nothing about! You can look and not see.' He was very chastened.

I went to have lunch at the Derby Hotel that used to supply our food, mainly in tins, but it had been converted into flats. The children's home was all offices, but I rang the bell and asked if I could look round. The only thing that was left from the home was a long, oak table that used to stand in the main hall.

India

After that year in the Isle of Man I was posted to India for two years from 1942 to 1944. We were in Bombay for three or four days when we first arrived in the country and I was then posted to Delhi. To get there we went on a rat-infested boat for a day and night to Karachi and then across the Sind Desert by train to Delhi. The train that had gone the week before had been held up by a band of Kurdish robbers. This time we had an armed escort. The Kurds arrived on horseback as the train crawled up a slope, the escort opened up on them and off they rode. It was just like a western film. We reported to this wireless experimental station outside Delhi at a place called Anamparbat. Whilst I was there, we had an outbreak of smallpox and I volunteered to be the only orderly for the smallpox patients. There were six and they and I were sealed off from everywhere else. The only people I saw for a month were my patients and the doctor. One of the patients nearly died but he did pull through. The Indian doctor said that once the outbreak was over he would like me to meet his family and I did. He had three sisters of 16, 18 and 23. They were Moslems and we ate with our fingers. After the meal I was expected to give a good belch to signal that I had enjoyed it, which I found difficult! The doctor's brother was an inspector of police and lived in a small palace – probably as the result of corruption. I hoped to see inside it but I never did.

Gadag

After the smallpox nursing I was allowed some leave and I decided to go and see my uncle at Gadag over a thousand miles away. He had gone out to India before the War and was in charge of a railway workshop. At the outbreak of War he had been made an army lieutenant but was still at Gadag. On the train I studied a map of India and spotted Poona. I decided to go there because when I was on the Isle of Man a friend of mine, Jackie Wells, was always saying, 'When I was in Poona.' This meant I had to change trains and had some trouble with my ticket, which was not for Poona! Poona had a wonderful station and a very impressive Imperial Bank of India building, which I managed to look round by going in and depositing five rupees. I had nowhere to stay and so I went to an army barracks and asked for a bed for the night. I was allocated this spare bed and, to my great surprise, in the bed opposite was Pat Meadows from Dover. He was in RAF intelligence photographing from aircraft. Then I went on to Gadag but arrived two days later than expected!

My uncle did not know how I was going to spend ten days there, but I had a wonderful time. I visited a prison, the hospital, the big railway station and a Swiss-US mission, the Basel Mission. There I saw people in this mud hut village making saris and started to go into the houses but was warned that I wouldn't be welcome. I didn't have any problems much to the surprise of the missionary with me who had never gone inside any of them. The hospital itself was made of brick. Whole families would come to the hospital and wait outside and in the village whole families including the children would be working.

I had asked one of the camp bearers to make me a white suit for the train journey to Gadag and the brass medical orderly 'dogs' that I usually wore on my lapels I put on my shoulders. My uncle took me by train to Hublie. My aunt's servant, Chinapapa, who was about 16 went in the carriage and I went on the footplate. When we got to Hublie we went around the bazaar, but the stallholders must have thought I was some sort of inspector on the make because whatever I touched they insisted I took without paying: guavas, mangoes, sugar cane etc. When we arrived home, Chinapapa said that he wouldn't go out shopping with me again! The train journey was about 140 miles and I had been on the footplate in a white suit. It was quite a mess but a wonderful experience.

I went to the hospital attached to the mission and made myself known and was invited to dinner. They told me to bring along my aunt and uncle who had never been there before. My uncle thought it was a bit much my being invited during a short visit when they had lived there for years and had never been. On the way there we passed a tall, well-built, naked holy man. My aunt was very embarrassed, but I had seen one before in Karachi. We had a great time at the dinner with a concert after the meal.

The Anglican Church had had to close at the beginning of the War because money had dried up. The clergyman was still there but the school and church had had to close, which was very sad.

A quick dip

For some reason the British Governor of the Punjab invited representatives of all the units in the Delhi area to his palace at Lahore. The names of all those interested went into a draw. My name went in, but didn't come out. The 50 chosen were told to meet in Connaught Circus the next morning. I asked my medical officer if I could go to the meeting place too, but he couldn't see the point as I was not going to Lahore. I explained that somebody might not turn up and I could go instead. He let me go and, sure enough, somebody didn't turn up. I called out that I was a reserve sent by Flight Lieutenant Rowley, my MO, which was stretching the truth a bit! So I was included.

We were given lunch by the Governor and then shown around this magnificent palace. I was at the back of the group and feeling very hot. I told the aide-de-camp that I was very hot and he said, 'Would you like a swim?' When I said that I didn't have any trunks, he told me to swim in the nude. 'Not on your life!' I said. Instead, he lent me some trunks, took me to the Governor's swimming pool and in I went. Then, who should walk in but the Governor and his wife! He asked the ADC what was going on who explained that he had told me to go in because I was so hot. The Governor walked out without saying anything. I wonder what he thought? It was just as well that I wasn't in the nude.

Taj Mahal

During my stay in Delhi I was anxious to visit the Taj Mahal at Agra, which was over 100 miles away but the MO said that he couldn't spare me for any leave, so I went overnight. I arrived late evening and saw the Taj Mahal by moonlight. I didn't see it until I went through this archway and then it hit me – the most beautiful thing I've ever seen. I stayed up all night, saw it again early morning and then went back to Delhi.

While I was in Delhi I had a second attack of malaria. I told the MO that I was all in; even though I was all right during the day I was having these intermittent fever attacks at night. In the evening we were performing *Journey's End* and I was in charge of props and playing Corporal Broughton in a big heavy overcoat in a dugout. General Wavell was in the audience. By the end of the play I had had it and got a lorry driver to take me to hospital. I went

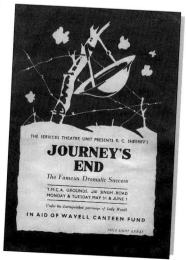

THE SERVICES THEATRE UNIT PRESENTS R. C. SHERRIFF'S

JOURNEY'S END

The Famous Dramatic Success

Y.M.C.A. GROUNDS, JAI SINGH-ROAD
MONDAY & TUESDAY MAY 31 & JUNE 1

Under the distinguished patronage of Lady Wavell

IN AID OF WAVELL CANTEEN FUND

PRICE EIGHT ANNAS

straight upstairs, found an empty bed and got in and told the driver to tell my doctor back at camp. When the doctor came he was furious with me for admitting myself without telling anybody and said there would be trouble over it. However, I replied that, if he made a fuss about me, I would have to tell about those times when people were taken ill at night and I diagnosed malaria, which was pretty obvious because of an enlarged spleen, called him and he authorised me to sign his name and admit the patients. That was the end of that!

While I was in hospital there were three cases of dysentery, which alarmed everybody. I gave it a lot of thought lying in my bed and told the doctor, a French major, that I had a theory. Visitors were bringing in bottles of lemonade from a lemonade factory across the road and I wondered whether that could be the cause. This was followed up and a carrier was found working in the factory. I was commended for it, which pleased me. I still get on edge when I see people drinking straight from bottles and I never do it myself.

A Dover Mowll

One day I was walking round Connaught Place, that is what I always called Connaught Circus, in Delhi, and there were two ladies walking in front of us. I said to my friend, 'One of those ladies comes from Dover.' 'How can you tell,' he asked. 'By her stature and walk.' I went up to her and asked, 'Excuse me, but is your name Miss Mowll?' 'Yes, it is. How do you know me?' she replied. Putting it as politely as I could, I said, 'Your stature reminds me of John Mowll in Dover who is our Commissioner for Scouts.' 'He is my uncle,' she laughed. We were introduced to her friend, a Miss Worsfold, from the well-known Dover family. These two ladies ran a maternity hospital in old Delhi and invited us to dinner. We had to get permission from the CO, because old Delhi was out of bounds, but we had a wonderful time. Miss Mowll's splayed feet were quite distinctive!

Stop the train!

I have had to pull the train communication cord four times in my life. The first was in India when a friend and I were leaving Karachi for Delhi and my friend left his kitbag on the platform. I pulled the communication cord and got into trouble. After the War, on the train from London to Dover, there were some football supporters who had had too much to drink and there was a rumpus when some of them wanted to get to the toilet; one lad ended up being trodden on. I shouted that I would pull the communication cord if they didn't stop and then did so. Fortunately, some rugby players sorted them out. On another occasion the train was leaving the platform in London when I heard a lady scream. She had got on the train with her young daughter but her son had been left behind on the platform and so I pulled the cord. The last time was when I was going from Dover to Canterbury. A drunken man got on at Dover and started fooling around with some girls. When he began to handle them, I pulled the cord and at Aylesham he was handcuffed and removed.

Stanley Matthews

When I was stationed at New Delhi my name came up on daily orders to play football, but I had never played football in my life for the simple reason that when

I was a boy I had a dropped muscle in my side that prevented me. It was operated on after I left school. I went to see the CO who was a South African Boer, a very strange man, and said, 'Sir, you'll have to take my name off the football team list.' 'You're playing,' he replied. I told him the reason but he insisted. I had no option. It was the medical and transport units playing the signals. I had no idea of football, of course, but for what it was worth I was playing on the wing against a fellow called Stanley Matthews (later, Sir Stanley) that I used to massage. It was quite a laugh. I was on the field and never touched the ball because he dribbled all around me! So, the only time I ever played organised football in kit was in Delhi against the great Stanley Matthews. Not many people can say that. Years later, a little boy that I picked up as an ambulance man in Queen's Avenue had been shot by an arrow on his way to cubs and had lost his eye. Afterwards I used to go to the house and take his artificial eye out and clean it because his parents didn't like doing it. He was very keen on football and so I said that I would get an autograph from Stanley Matthews. I wrote twice but never received a reply even though we had been quite friendly in Delhi.

One day a friend and I climbed Kutab Minar, which is 11 miles south of Delhi in old Delhi. It is a huge tower 246 feet high covered in writings chiselled into it, built to celebrate a victory by some emperor in the 13th century. It took 40 years to build. When I got to the top I threw my Air Force cap all the way down and was going to collect it when I got to the bottom again, but it fell onto a ledge halfway down and I lost it. I really got into trouble about that.

When I was in Calcutta I went to see the banyan tree. Before 1940 7,000 men sheltered under it – it covered 20 acres. It was the biggest tree I had ever seen in my life.

Allahabad

There was a spot of trouble at Delhi when a Major Craig, who was on the Mess Committee, resigned because he said I caused too much trouble. I had to go to Delhi HQ with the MO who had some business there and whilst I was there I saw the Catering Officer and asked him to have a look at our catering situation. He telephoned my people who found out that I was behind it and they went mad. Anyway, the Catering Officer came, but, of course, special arrangements were made and I objected backed up by some sergeants. The major, a nasty piece of work, said that he would get me posted. I was a 'disturbing influence.' I was posted to Allahabad. When I got to the train, there was no sleeping compartment for me, which had to be provided under King's Regulations for an overnight journey, so I returned to camp. This was a week before Christmas and I had a nice week off before I was posted to Allahabad again. When I got there I was told it was a wonderful place because you could have trips with the RAF pilots, but I was the only one who took advantage of it. I went to Cawnpore on one occasion but found that the plane wasn't returning, it was going to be scrapped, so I was stranded and due on duty at 6pm and I had the poison cupboard key in my pocket. I told the CO my plight and he arranged for one of the planes going to Allahabad the next day to go immediately. I managed to get on duty by 6.30pm!

Acting on the spur of the moment sometimes gets me into trouble. I remember seeing a camel on the airfield at Allahabad and said to my friends, Frank Lenham

The camel ride

and Chalky White, 'Let's have a ride.' I checked that no aircraft were due to fly in and out and then we rode this camel across the airfield. I had to go before the CO but I didn't get charged – on that occasion.

When I was in the sick quarters at Bamrolli – a converted bungalow – next door lived a police inspector named Singh. His son and three other boys went round the airfield collecting up cartridges, which they pushed into a long tube and then hit it. The son got badly burned. I rushed out and put this lad into a bath of tepid water until the ambulance arrived. Mr Singh was very grateful. He owned a lot of mango groves and said that I could collect as many mangoes as I wanted. So I collected them, boiled them, let the juice cool and then mixed it with sherry and gave it to the patients in the sick quarters. We soon had plenty of visitors looking for a glass of this concoction!

Bamrolli had a little drive where you came in one way and out the other. One evening I saw two oxen pulling a cart with a driver who was fast asleep. My philosophy in life is to help other people at all times, but on this occasion that went to the wind. I caught hold of the oxen's reins and took them up the drive and sent them back the way they had come. Goodness knows where they ended up and what the driver thought. I have never forgiven myself for doing it.

Sacred cow

One day I got a lift down to old Allahabad, which was really out of bounds. I was dropped just outside and I arranged to be picked up half an hour later. I noticed this boy walking along with a school atlas in his hand. There was also a cow in the road. Cows, of course, are sacred in India. The cow snatched the boy's atlas as he passed. I called out, 'Don't worry my little friend, I'll get it back for you.' Then I realised that this cow had one big horn and one crumpled horn. I thought, Jack be careful. I went round the other side of the cow, retrieved the atlas and

34

gave it back to the boy. The next thing I knew, I was going up in the air. I had been tossed! When I landed, people tried to lift me but I told them to leave me alone until I had checked myself over. There was no blood. Fortunately, only the crumpled horn had been used. The sharp horn would have finished me. I waited for the ambulance and was taken to hospital where the surgeon had a good laugh. Nothing was broken but I was very badly bruised and had to stay in hospital for three days. While I was there I acquired a shooting stick that I kept right through India and Burma and brought it back home. I still have it. When I was released and got back to my HQ there was a 'reception committee' waiting for me and they sang the as I walked in!

In Allahabad an Indian corporal used to take me out and show me how to handle snakes. That stood me in good stead when I went to Burma and years later in Australia.

Monkey nuts

At one time I was in charge of a number of men going on convalescence. We left Delhi by train for Dehra-Dun in the foothills of the Western Himalayas. We transferred to lorries in order to get to Chakrata and a number of men were sick from the very windy roads. A lot of them had been suffering from sprue – something like diarrhoea with white frothy stools and you lose a lot of weight. Early one morning I came upon a school of monkeys in the pepal trees. By clapping I moved them on to walnut trees and they started shaking the trees bringing down the nuts. The boys in the hut wondered where I had got the walnuts. It was an interesting station. There was a boy who complained of pain. I examined him and diagnosed an enlarged spleen. I took him in a truck to the hospital a couple of miles away. When I got there they told me about a black panther that had killed a child. I thought they were mistaken, as there were cows outside our hut grazing peacefully. Anyway I walked down the valley in the evening and saw a pair of black eyes. I ran for it and got away. Later the CO shot it, but the people from the bazaar were annoyed because he had shot it but only wounded it. They didn't want it killed at all but had had to finish it off. The CO demanded the panther skin, which was all pegged out. They raided our hut for revenge, cut open the kit bags and made off with all sorts of stuff. I didn't lose anything because I was the only person with a tin trunk, not a kit bag. There was another panic that night with two bats flying round the hut. I've never seen men so scared!

At one stage I was attached to a small Canadian unit as a medical orderly but with no medical officer. I had one lad who was very sick and I couldn't diagnose what was wrong with him. I didn't think that it was appendicitis, it could have been colic but I wasn't happy so I said to the officer that I was going to send the patient to Cuttack, which was 70 miles away. 'Oh no you won't,' he said. I didn't let it go at that and told him that he was no medical officer whereas I had a certain amount of medical training and, if he didn't take my advice, I would pack my bags and go back to Calcutta. I had my way! After three months the unit closed down and the principal medical officer in the area said, 'You're the man who wanted to see some action and asked to go to the Khyber Pass. Well, we've got a place for you. You're going to Burma.'

Burma

I was in Burma serving with 60 Mobile Field Hospital during the siege and stayed for two years. It was blooming hot. As many people died there from dysentery and other illnesses as from the war. The Japanese poisoned the water at one stage and we had to have water dropped to us. That's when I realised how important water is when you only had a cup of water per day to use for everything! On another occasion Vera Lynn came out to entertain the troops. When her concert finished I went up to her and said, 'Excuse me, but I'm in charge of the amputees in the camp hospital and it would be marvellous if you could come and see them.' She said that she would, but I pointed out that it might cause a bit of trouble. Her manager told me to contact him if I got into trouble. The sergeant said that I was for the high jump because the powers that be had a meal laid on for her and she was nearly an hour late from giving

Jack in Burma

this impromptu concert in the ward. The adjutant sent me to the CO and I said, 'Well Sir, whatever you decide to do, I have a contact and I will tell him what has happened. Vera Lynn came out to sing for the troops and that is what she was doing.' Nothing ever happened!

A life and death situation occurred one day when Corporal Eric Downs got into difficulties in the Chindwin River and would have been swept away. Eight of us formed a life chain to save him and were commended for it.

Whilst in Burma I climbed Mount Deoban with five others. Native bearers carried our kit. We covered a lot of ground going through elephant grass, which was higher than a man and a number of leeches attached themselves to us. We had to light matches to get them to drop off. On another occasion I did a stupid thing by taking a short cut through some grass to get to the cinema in Rangoon. In the cinema I thought my leg felt funny, took a look and my shoe was full of blood from this leech on my leg!

The Russian Order

While I was in Rangoon in 1946, Alf Curd, the Dover Superintendent of St John Ambulance had received my Service Ribbon of the Order of St John for 15 years service and sent it out to me – my war service counted – so I put it on my jacket and the Medical Officer asked me what it was and I said it was the Russian Order. 'What was that for,' he said and I replied, 'For rushin' about!' He got quite annoyed and I told him what it really was. 'You're not allowed to wear that,' he said. 'Oh yes I am,' I replied, 'the King is Head of the Order.' He sent me to the adjutant and I told him that it was a recognised ribbon for 15 years service to the Order of St John of which the King was head. I stuck to my guns and they made enquiries and found that they couldn't do anything about it!

In trouble again

In Rangoon Air Vice Marshal Vincent came in to the sick quarters complaining of dysentery, but I thought he had no more dysentery than I had; he had come for a rest! We didn't get off to a good start. The first morning I asked him to fold his mosquito net and he thought I should do it, but I refused. If he didn't want to do such things he should have brought his bearer with him! He didn't like being on his own in the officers' ward but, after one day, Air Commodore Smith joined him. I was looking after the officers and had to take their meals up to them, but he always turned meals down saying he would have them later. It was quite a trek up and down stairs with this food and I had had enough, so I decided that if he didn't eat his meal when I took it up first time then I would take it up cold when he did want it. It was the usual performance and when I took up the cold meal he complained. I said that I had other people to worry about and he should have brought his bearer with him. He called for the adjutant who called the CO, Wing Commander Peall, who then sent for me. 'You can't do this, Jack,' he said, 'He is the commander of our group.' So I asked to be taken off the officers' ward and I was, but the Sister asked for me back. Fortunately, Air Vice Marshal Vincent left after five days. I was always in trouble!

The Mountbattens

When the present Countess Mountbatten came to Dover Town Hall I was presented to her as a character of the town. I told her how I had been present in Burma at a march past attended by her mother and father when it was tipping down with rain but Lord and Countess Mountbatten had taken their raincoats off for the march past and, of course, all the other generals and dignitaries had to follow suit and got soaked. At the Town Hall I asked if I could have a photograph taken with the Countess and she agreed. It came out so well that I sent one to her and

Countess Mountbatten at Dover Town Hall, 1985

asked her to autograph it for me and she did.

In Burma and India I was able to see at first hand some of the voluntary work done by the Order of St John there. The efficient and compassionate manner in which the late Countess Mountbatten dealt with the refugee problem was a revelation.

Burton Bros.

In Rangoon at the end of the War we were dealing with British prisoners released by the Japanese. Amongst them were two Burton brothers of Burtons the Tailors. These poor devils were just skeletons and when I went into the ward they would bow, as they had had to do to the Japanese. They couldn't break the habit. These prisoners would only stay with us a few days before moving on and were nourished on grapefruit and chicken. Much later, in 1954, when I was taking scouts to the World Jamboree, I was asking for donations to help pay for the trip. I ran a big dance at the Co-op Hall to raise funds. I went to Burtons in Dover and asked for a donation, but they said their HQ gave money to the scouts centrally. So I wrote to Burtons' Head Office, asked for a donation and said that they might remember me from those days in Rangoon. I received a £50 cheque!

I saw enormous suffering and tragedy at close hand during the War years. Looking back I can hardly believe it all happened. What a terrible waste of life it all was.

Chapter 3

POST WAR AND A NEW JOB

I was demobbed in March 1946 and returned to Dover. Most of the bombing of the town was done before I went, so I wasn't too surprised at the state of it when I came back after the War. The Pier District, the sea front, Pencester Road and the St James' area had been severely damaged. There was a Mrs Wright who lived on

Bomb damage: Technical College, Ladywell

the corner of Pencester Road and Maison Dieu Road. Her house was hit three times and she was so relieved when she wasn't hit by bombs or shells. I went to church to give thanks for being spared and that the War was over and I was greatly surprised by ladies in church with no hats. I was also surprised by people

Bomb damage: Ladywell Police Station

Bomb damage: Stembrook

queuing for ice cream in the winter – before the War you only thought about ice cream in the summer! Telegram boys in their pillbox hats were a lovely sight. The sea front defences had been cleared but all the bomb and shell damaged houses were still there – and were for some time.

Bomb damage: Snargate Street

Last shell to fall on Dover at corner of Church Street and Castle Street

County Ambulance Service

Although our house and shop had been bombed, the bake house was still standing and my brother had carried on baking during the War. My mother had died in 1942 at Waldershare House, which had become a wartime hospital, and Dad remarried at the end of the War. When he died in 1947, everything went to my stepmother. The miller offered to set up my brother in business in Tower Hamlets in Dawes' old bakery. I went with him for about a year, but I was more interested in first aid. So when, in 1948, the National Health Service took over most of the ambulance duties performed by St John, I wrote to the County Medical Officer and asked if there were any vacancies for a county ambulance driver. There weren't any then but he told me to apply when the next Dover vacancy came up. When it did there were eight applicants and I got in as a county ambulance driver and stayed for 29? years. I was never interested in promotion because that would mean I wouldn't do first aid as part of the job.

I'm still at it. Only recently I was on my way to Ashford Hospital for an appointment and there had been a car crash with four ladies injured. I told my nephew to stop the car. He wanted to go on in case we missed my appointment but I insisted. We had allowed half an hour extra time anyway. I jumped out of the car and checked out all four ladies. I thought one had fractured ribs, another concussed, another had a bruised face and one was all right. One of the ladies stopped me in the town a day or two later and so I asked what had happened when they were taken to hospital; it was just as I had diagnosed! The two men in the van that had hit them had abandoned the van and vanished.

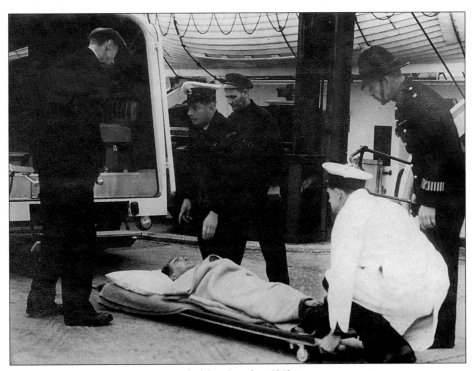

An injured survivor 1949

42

Don't move me

I had only been in the ambulance service for about four months and was going on duty after visiting my mother's grave. I was driving a small Corgi motor-scooter when a motorcyclist came along at speed, ran into me and knocked me against the wall at the bottom of Chalky Lane, where Connaught Road joins Frith Road. Everybody wanted to move me, but I told them not to until the ambulance arrived because I had no sensation in my legs. My spine could have been fractured. In fact I had pieces broken off three lumbar vertebrae. The doctor said afterwards that I could have been in real trouble if I had been moved without following strict procedures. I was in hospital for three weeks. Whilst I was there, my sister gave birth to a daughter in the ward upstairs and sent down a message saying that they were both well and the baby had black hair like a lavatory brush!

More deliveries

During my years with the County Ambulance Service I delivered, or helped to deliver, several babies. Unable to get a midwife I found myself in the back of the ambulance with an expectant mother, Mrs Scott, whom we had picked up from Old Park Barracks. The husband, a sergeant-major, came with us. Going down Folkestone Hill the mother said, 'I think the baby's coming.' 'Not to worry,' I reassured her, 'I'm used to this!' The sergeant-major fainted and fell off his seat into the gangway. So, in order to deliver the baby I had to stand on him. It felt so good delivering the baby and cleaning it up. The mother asked what she had got and I replied, 'It's a teapot.' She smiled and wanted to name the baby after me; so I told her to use my middle name, John. During my service I spent a week in the hospital maternity ward. I was only present for one delivery and that was Mrs

Ambulancemen: Bill Godsmark, Billy Knott, Ronnie Vowles, Bert Baker, Wally Pascal, Reg Reader, and in front, Stanley Boyd and Jack

Marian Howard's baby on 2 March 1973. I held her hand and said, 'Not to worry, all will be well.' The baby was born and named John Robert. He is a father himself now. There were several more deliveries while I was an ambulance man and some were very difficult.

Pet trouble

I had a lovely little slate grey kitten, part Siamese and part Persian, that I called Imphal, named after a place in Burma. I took it with me on my shoulder when I went shopping and when I went to the St John Ambulance cadets' meetings. I also had a pet hare that I called Mymeo, also named after a place in Burma. He used to come indoors and sit on my lap. One evening, when I was on standby for an ambulance callout – for which we were paid half a crown – Mymeo chewed through my telephone cable. It was after 10 o'clock. I telephoned the exchange from my neighbour's house but they couldn't repair it until the next morning and so I telephoned the ambulance station. I asked them to come and get me if I was needed, but they would only need me if they were called out to an emergency themselves and wouldn't have time to knock me up. To cut a long story short, I told them that I would sleep in my front bedroom with a long cord tied to my ankle and the cord would dangle out of the bedroom window. All they had to do was to give it a good pull! Around midnight I felt myself being pulled down the bed. I got dressed and dashed to the ambulance station just in time for another emergency at Buckland Bridge where somebody had driven into the river.

In trouble again

When a visiting aircraft carrier was moored off Shakespeare Beach I was one of those invited on board. Boats took visitors to and fro. I was due on duty at 10pm but there was plenty of time. My niece was with me and we were having a wonderful time. Then I checked when the next boat was taking people off –
10pm! I couldn't get back in time. I arrived for duty at 10.45pm and was reprimanded. I was in trouble again when we were called out for an appendicitis case on a cargo ship in the Channel. There was a rough sea and the doctor didn't fancy it. I offered to go with him but the ambulance station told me not to as it wasn't my job. I went anyway, thinking it was the right thing to do in the circumstances. Sometimes I was praised for my actions even though strictly it wasn't my job. In 1955 I was commended for helping to save the life of a patient suffering from polio at the Noah's Ark Isolation Hospital. The patient was in an iron lung when he stopped breathing. The other two ambulance

Jack and Frank 'Atty' Pearce
with Naranco survivor 1959

men said that it wasn't our job, but I pulled him out of the lung, massaged him, got him breathing again and put him back!

As an ambulance man or first aider you often have to deal with the relatives as well as the injured and this can be difficult. I remember a cot death and when the father came home he went berserk.

Despite all this, I thoroughly enjoyed the work and found it satisfying. I would even change shifts to get on to the crash vehicle duty. I liked making diagnoses. I suppose that today I would be a paramedic. You could not be callous, but you had to steel yourself for some nasty situations. I always felt upset when children were killed or injured.

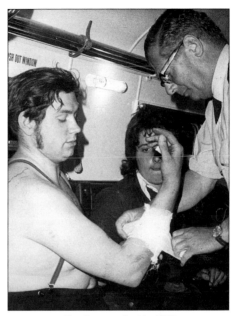

Tending a patient in 1972

Whipper-in

The army barracks in Dover had a beagle pack and I got interested and went out with them. When that pack disbanded, Mr Marsh, who was involved with the dogs, suggested that I supported the beagle pack at Ringwould where he was the master of hounds. From 1947 to 1949 I was a beagles whipper-in for the Ringwould pack and in all that time we never caught a hare; however, it was good

Jack as a whipper-in with Hon. Mrs Bruce in 1949

The Ringwould beagles pack

exercise. About a week before one Christmas Mr Mowll, a great supporter, persuaded Mr Marsh to go riding even though Mr Marsh hadn't ridden for a few years. While he was out Mr Marsh lost his false teeth and couldn't find them, which was a real problem because he needed them to blow the horn on the Boxing Day hunt! His wife asked all the local churches to announce that some false teeth had been lost in the countryside and asked for them to be handed in if found. Twelve pairs were handed in and Mrs Marsh spent Christmas Day trying to get a pair to fit! When I saw him on Boxing Day with these ill-fitting teeth I laughed and laughed! My favourite dog was called Dover and when the pack was disbanded he was bought by an Italian count. I had one of the beagles for a pet.

Up to tricks

I was often up to harmless tricks. I remember dressing up as a tramp for a tramps' supper sometime in the 1960s and on my way I went into the police station and asked for food, but was promptly shown the door!

Dressed for a tramps' supper in the 1960s

Chapter 4

SCOUTING

Scouting has played a big part in my life. The movement began when General Baden-Powell returned from the Boer War in 1902 and wrote a book for young soldiers called, Aids to Scouting. Lads who got hold of this book wanted to put words into action: there was camping, cooking, knotting, signalling, observation, tracking, map reading, self discipline, duty to God and the king. Of course, this was before radio, television, computers and the like. Leaders were required and had to be trained. In 1907 an experimental camp was held on Brownsea Island in Poole Harbour where twenty boys of different backgrounds worked and played together: it was successful. That was the start of the great brotherhood, which spread like wildfire across Great Britain and the world. The first issue of the weekly paper, The Scout, came out in July 1908, price 1d. I have the second issue and many more that followed. They make interesting reading. Just before King Edward VII died in 1910, he asked Baden-Powell if he would leave the army and devote his time and energy to scouting. This he did and in 1920 at Richmond Park, 6000 scouts from 21 countries surrounded B-P, lifted him shoulder high around the arena and acclaimed him as Chief Scout of the world, an honour he prized above all others. B-P was the most decorated man in Great Britain with 26 orders of which 20 were foreign, six honorary degrees and the freedom of many capitals. He wrote 34 books and many pamphlets.

Part I.

Price 4d. net

SCOUTING FOR BOYS BY B-P

LIEUT. GEN. BADEN POWELL C.B.

PUBLISHED BY HORACE COX,
WINDSOR HOUSE, BREAM'S BUILDINGS, LONDON E.C.

Scouting in Dover

I have been told that there were 23 troops in Dover in 1917, although I haven't been able to verify it. In 1918 the Scouts' Association was commended for its work during the War and the Dover and St Margaret's Sea Scouts were commended by the War Office for their valuable work coastguard watching, using semaphore flags and passing on messages. The first troop in Dover was 1st Dover, Charlton. The curate, Revd. Cobbe, was so keen that he formed the troop in 1907 before scouting was officially launched. The second was Dover Sea Scouts, which had three whalers; one of its first officers was Mr Sharp of Sharp and Enright followed by Coggy Pearce and Dutchy Holland. The 3rd Dover, St Martin's, was formed in 1908. Mr Tom Eaves, who was a popular master at St Martin's School and scoutmaster of the local troop, was killed in the First World War. Eaves Hall, the Dover Scout HQ, was built behind Markland Road in his memory and opened in 1934. Money was raised by 'selling' bricks at £1 each, which would be refunded later, but most people did not bother to reclaim the money.

Subsequently properties were built alongside and the residents described it as New Road; however, the Corporation decided to call it Eaves Road. One person objected but was overruled.

Jack, 23rd Dover Sea Scouts, 1924

Scouting has played an important part in character building for the youngsters of Dover for decades and I hope that all have become good citizens. There have been troops of scouts at the Gordon Boys' Orphanage, the County School, now the Boys' Grammar School and Dover College.

I joined the Sea Scouts in 1924 and my first duty was at the Dover War Memorial on Sunday, 5 November 1924, when it was unveiled by Sir Roger Keyes. There were crowds around it as far as the eye could see. Then there was the Remembrance Service on the following Saturday. Except for the War years I have attended every Remembrance Parade since.

World Jamboree

I only lasted six months in the Sea Scouts before I left and joined Charlton Scouts. When I was 18 years old the World Scout Jamboree was being held in England – in the Midlands somewhere – and I wanted to go, but my father said no. However, I did help those scouts arriving at Dover on their way to the jamboree. I went out on a tug, the *Lady Savil*, to take some Jamaican scouts off a cargo ship carrying bananas. We took two policemen with us. There was a stowaway on board who was handcuffed by the policemen and I think the scouts were more interested in that than looking at Dover Castle! One of the lads asked he if could be a pen pal of mine, his name was Percy Walcott. The following day I was helping again on Admiralty Pier, looking for a Hungarian milk churn on a ferry, but I couldn't find it. The gangway was blocked, but instead of waiting I jumped off the side of the boat. At the same time the rope from the crane unloading the luggage broke and I was hit on the head by a heavy suitcase. I was in Dover Hospital for a month with a fractured skull and then went to an aunt in Gravesend for a month to convalesce. I couldn't remember a thing for a while. So, not only did I not go to the jamboree, but I was out of action for two months!

Baden-Powell

In 1930 I became an Assistant Scoutmaster. In 1932 in *The Scouter* a special weekend camp was announced at which the Chief Scout, Lord Baden-Powell, would be present; there was a competition for assistant scoutmasters, which I was by then, and we had to write an essay about why we would like to meet the Chief Scout. We also had to be 20, which I was. So I entered and I got a place. There were 32 of us camping with Baden-Powell at Gilwell Park. In the morning after breakfast, he walked across to us, so I said, 'Here comes the Chief. We ought to

Jack, Charlton Rover Scout, aged 16 in 1928

Baden-Powell

stand up.' We did so, but Baden-Powell said, 'Sit down brothers, I am one of you.' I told him that I had not been introduced to him the previous evening at the campfire because I was a baker and had been busy baking. I asked him if it were possible to see his caravan. He agreed and took me to it. 'There you are. It's all yours. Have a look at it,' he said. I opened the door and this Labrador dog jumped out. He laughed and said, 'Always go careful, careful.' I have told this story to several groups of scouts over the years and at Whitfield, as I went out, a scout said to me, 'Careful, careful!'

In 1955, I persuaded General Elliot to come on a training course with me at Gilwell Park in London, which greatly increased his knowledge of scouting as he was our Commissioner. In doing so I was also fulfilling a promise that I made to Lord Baden-Powell in 1932 that I would return to Gilwell and I did.

I became Scoutmaster to the Dover 1st in 1935 and Group Scoutmaster of my troop, the 6th Dover Westcliff Western Heights in 1936. After the War I became Scoutmaster of the Dover 3rd and Assistant District Commissioner (Seniors) from 1951 to 1961.

Waldershare Park

In 1935 I wrote to Lord Guilford asking permission to take physically handicapped scouts, the 8th Dover, camping in Waldershare Park. The reply was that, because of damage, no camping was allowed. I wrote again saying that, if we were allowed to camp, nobody would know that we had been afterwards. Permission was granted! Whilst Scoutmaster Bernard Wood was cooking the dinner – it was lamb stew with dumplings, I remember – I took a couple of scouts to collect dead wood for the fire. When I came back there was a man that I took to be the farmer talking to the boys. He asked if we were enjoying ourselves and I replied, 'Yes, thanks to the old earl who gave us permission to camp here.' The man replied, 'I am the old earl!' I wished that the ground could have opened up and swallowed me. Lord and Lady Guilford were very good to the scouts. On one occasion at Waldershare we went into an area called The Wilderness collecting

A scout celebration, 1950

conkers and chestnuts and observing a woodpecker. We crept closer and then saw a stoat with a rabbit that it had paralysed. It was a once in a lifetime thing for 'townies' and what you would only see now on television rather than for real. In 1952 or thereabouts we were out in Waldershare Park and met the wood reeve, Mr Fraser, who gave the boys a lot of knowledge about trees. One of the lads could eventually identify all sorts of trees in winter or summer. There isn't a tree badge for scouts, but it is part of the nature badge.

At this time I also helped with the group of physically handicapped scouts managed by Bernard Wood and used to fetch a handicapped boy from Devonshire Road, pulling him in his homemade soapbox barrow to Market Street on scout nights.

Boy Scout Hymn

The Boy Scout hymn isn't known now but it's a lovely hymn and used to be sung at scout services and especially on St George's Day.

> *Now as I start upon my chosen way,*
> *In all I do, my thoughts, my work, my play,*
> *Grant as I promise, courage new for me*
> *To be the best, the best that I can be.*
>
> *Help me to keep my honour shining bright,*
> *May I be loyal in the hardest fight,*
> *Let me be able for my task, and then,*
> *To earn a place among my fellow men.*
>
> *Open my eyes to see things as I should,*
> *That I may do my daily turn of good,*
> *Let me be ready, waiting for each need*
> *To keep me clean in thought and word and deed.*
>
> *So as I journey on my chosen way,*
> *In all I do, my thought, my work, my play,*
> *Grant as I promise, courage new for me*
> *To be the best, the best that I can be.*

Operation Alpine

In 1951 I took 32 scouts to the World Jamboree in Austria and in 1952 Lord Rowallan presented me with the Medal of Merit and in 1954 I led a group of 32 senior scouts to the Scout's international campsite at Kandersteg in Switzerland. It was called Operation Alpine and the scouts wore a district scarf of light and dark blue with a badge of the Dover coat of arms on the back. One senior scout dropped out and so I invited another, Geoffrey Groombridge, to go who lived in Avenue Road and whose father was unemployed. They had no spare money but I said that it wouldn't cost them anything; we had raised the money for the trip. The lad had a wonderful time.

We travelled in an Ayers coach with George Ayers driving. It was the

World Jamboree, 1951

company's first trip abroad. We did some sightseeing on the way, staying overnight in a Paris school. Kandersteg is 3870 feet above sea level with a chalet accommodating 170, plus camping grounds for another thousand. We stayed in the chalet. During the nine days we did three strenuous climbs in beautiful scenery going up to 9,000 feet. I was used to handling snakes in India where I was shown how to pick them up safely. During a climb I saw this snake and picked it up and said, 'Look what I've got'. Then I thought that was a stupid thing to do and put it back! We also had some sightseeing trips by bus, rail and lake steamer. It was a wonderful trip for the boys and me.

Climbing

My love of mountains began in the RAF. After the War I climbed on the Brown Slabs in the Lake District in 1954. One of my scouts, Norman Woolhouse, started his climbing then and became an experienced mountaineer and a professor of biology. All my senior scouts did well for themselves. Whichever country I've been in I've always wanted to go up into the mountains. In the main I've gone by cable car or chair lift and then walked around, but when I went in 1951 to the World Scout Jamboree at Bad Ischl in Austria a little lad aged 15, called Wilfried Emden, was fascinated by my laugh and was always inviting me to go to his camp. Every year afterwards he would write and ask when I would return to his beautiful country, Austria. Ten years later he asked me yet again and I went. I arrived at Wilfried's chalet and next morning we set off early to reach this mountain hut and stayed in it over night. He said, 'In the morning we climb.' During the jamboree I had taken my 32 scouts climbing and so Wilfried thought that I was a proper climber! The only climbing I had done was with scouts on the

Brown Slabs in the Lake District. There was Wilfried and five others who had all this mountaineering gear and there was I saying that I couldn't do it! But I had to. I was scared but it was great. The mountain was called the Godfather.

On another occasion I took some scouts to the Lake District for their adventure badge. When we were out rambling I asked one of them to pretend to fall and break his leg to see if the rest could cope with the accident. He acted the part so well that when a man overtook us he offered to help. He was a doctor and I had to take him aside and explain that it was only an exercise!

Surprise

I had lots of fun taking scouts on jaunts of one sort or another and surprising them. I remember organising a Saturday hike in 1958. I told the scouts to bring their camping kit and to meet at the Clock Tower. I told just one boy to bring his swimming trunks. We walked to the Granville Dock where I asked a man with a motorboat for a lift. I had, of course, hired it in advance. He took us to St Margaret's Bay where we made three attempts to land. Finally, we made use of the boy with the swimming trunks who got into the water and pulled us in. We camped at a farm and went back the following night.

Scout shows

The Dover Scout shows were put on in the Co-op Hall in Maison Dieu Road that is now used by the Royal Mail. Alfred Haynes produced them in alternate years. For *Great Oaks*, a play written by Ralph Reader, I said that I would help but would not take a part. However, everybody said that I was the only one who could play the mad major! One of my problems was that I didn't always stick to the script and ad libbed. This girl had to faint on stage and on the first night I said, 'Right, to recover the head must be low and the legs high,' and promptly got a chair and put this girl's legs up which meant that the audience could see her underwear! I didn't do that again. I was in a couple of other scout plays.

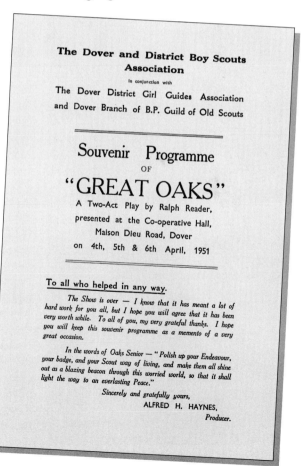

The Dover and District Boy Scouts Association

In conjunction with

The Dover District Girl Guides Association and Dover Branch of B.P. Guild of Old Scouts

Souvenir Programme

OF

"GREAT OAKS"

A Two-Act Play by Ralph Reader, presented at the Co-operative Hall, Maison Dieu Road, Dover on 4th, 5th & 6th April, 1951

To all who helped in any way.

The Show is over — I know that it has meant a lot of hard work for you all, but I hope you will agree that it has been very worth while. To all of you, my very grateful thanks. I hope you will keep this souvenir programme as a memento of a very great occasion.

In the words of Oaks Senior — " Polish up your Endeavour, your badge, and your Scout way of living, and make them all shine out as a blazing beacon through this worried world, so that it shall light the way to an everlasting Peace."

Sincerely and gratefully yours,
ALFRED H. HAYNES,
Producer.

I also went to a Ralph Reader Gang Show in London. On the way there had been a car accident and we stopped. We got one man out of a lorry but he was dead. Another chap had a broken arm and somebody else was concussed. We left in a hurry so that we didn't miss the show but I was covered in blood! I found out later that the injured people in the car were policemen transporting three boys to a Borstal.

Guild of Old Scouts

A guild of old scouts was formed after the War but it eventually petered out. We did have Lord Peter Baden-Powell, B-P's son, at our first annual dinner in 1952. I sat near him and asked how he got on with his father. Lord Peter replied that B-P was a good father, very kind but determined. When B-P saw Peter each morning he would ask, 'Peter, which way is the wind blowing? What can you see on the hedge?' He was always being questioned to stretch him educationally. B-P could not get him into the army and so Peter went to South Africa and joined the police. Peter was very nice but he hadn't got what his father had. Unfortunately, father expected more of Peter than he had in him.

Jack on his way to Windsor, 1982

President Jack

I came out of the Scouts in 1961 after being Assistant District Commissioner for ten years because the St John Ambulance Superintendent retired and there was nobody to take on that position and they asked me to do it. So I was doing both jobs and it wore me out. My doctor told me I had to stop some of my activities, so I gave up scouting and stayed in St John. But in 1981 I was in Buckland Hospital and read that eight boys were going to Kandersteg in Switzerland. The newspaper report said that this was the first time scouts from Dover had been. I couldn't have that because I had taken 32 boys there in 1954 and so I wrote to the Express pointing this out. The press contacted me and I said that years ago I had known all the scouts in Dover and everybody else. The Dover District Commissioner at that time was Mrs Rook, a lovely lady, and she wrote to me in 1981 and invited me to be their Vice President. In 1982 I was awarded the Silver Acorn and was

Jack as Dover District Scout President, 1999 with Richard Carter (Commissioner), Jonathan Veness and James Morris of 6th Dover Whitfield

then invited to the Chapel Royal, Windsor Castle for the St George's Day Service with the Chief Scout. In 1982 I was also asked to be President succeeding the Earl of Guilford and I've been President ever since. I get more invitations to visit troops than I can handle and I attend scouting events as a first aider. I've kept my first aid qualifications up to date and have been a first aid badge examiner for scouts and guides for many years.

Church

When I left the scouts I started going to St Mary's Church and I still attend. Before that I went to St Martin's Church when I was in charge of the senior scouts that met at St Martin's and before the War, when I was running the troop at the Western Heights, I attended the Western Heights garrison church.

Reunion

In 1950 I had taken St Martin's Senior Scouts camping for two weeks at an adventure camp at Keswick in the Lake District. In 1998 we held a reunion at the home of Norman Woolhouse in Maison Dieu Road, one of those who went. Not everybody could make it, but those who did were: James Brown, a retired Lieutenant Colonel, Laurie Reynolds, a retired head teacher, Richard Francis, a retired teacher, Douglas Reader, a former director of Littlewoods Pools, and David King, chairman of Dover Scout Association. Most of us hadn't met for 48 years, so we had plenty to talk and laugh about!

Adventure camp at Keswick in the Lake District 1950

Reunion in 1998 of the 3rd Dover Senior Scouts camp, 1950:
Norman Woolhouse, Jack, James Brown, Laurie Reynolds, Douglas Reader and Richard Francis

Chapter 5

MEMBER OF ST JOHN

I have belonged to the St John movement since I was 18. My mother said to me that if I was in the Scout movement then I should have first aid knowledge. She told me to join the St John Ambulance but I said that I didn't have time. 'You'll have to make time,' she said. So I went to the Royal Victoria Hospital Outpatients' Department and joined the St John in May 1930 and I'm still in it now. I didn't do too much in my first year, about 12 drills and a couple of duties. I wasn't very keen. In the days before Christmas, 1931, I was busy with calls. First, I had to go to Tower Hamlets where a man, who had stolen some Christmas money, had gassed himself and I had to deal with it. We got him on to a stretcher in the ambulance and I gave artificial respiration as we went along, but a dog ran across the road; our driver braked hard and I fell on top of the man. The pressure on his body resuscitated him! Then I had to attend to this boy who had been run over by a lorry at the bottom of Wyndham Road and taken into the local Co-op. His screams were terrible. On Boxing Day I got a call while I was eating my dinner. Mr Fox, the ambulance officer, came for me; I left my dinner and went to this car accident on Castle Hill where two people were badly injured. After all this I realised that I didn't have sufficient first aid knowledge and I've been keen on first aid ever since.

State duties

I was an active member of the organisation for 67 years. Recently, I received a special certificate from the Superintendent-in-Chief and was made an Honorary Life Member. I became a Corporal and then a Cadet Officer in 1935 and took part in my first London duty in the same year, the Silver Jubilee of King George V.

Jack promoted to Cadet Officer 1935
Standing (from left) Mr Williams, Bob Marsh, George Reason, Mr McKeen, Bob Winter, unknown, unknown, Jack; Seated (from left) Dot Saunders, Mrs Curd, Mr Marsh, Mr Fox, Dr Hamilton, Alderman Gore, Dr Nichol, Mr Abbott, Mr Wiggins, Mrs Edser, unknown

Since then I have been on duty at 14 royal and state occasions including the funeral of George V, the coronations of George VI and Elizabeth II, the funerals of George VI, Churchill and Mountbatten and the wedding of Charles and Diana. In 1937 I became Cadet Superintendent – cadets are boys and girls from 8 to 16 years who learn first aid and assist adult members in their duties. I have countless memories of weekend camps. On one occasion, whilst camping with the cadets at Folkestone Warren, a plane crashed there and we helped rescue the pilot. The *Dover Express* commended us for the part we played.

Dover's St John contingent to the 1953 Coronation duty
Standing (from left): Mrs E Francis, Sgt W Gratton, Sgt A Pullen, Sgt F Jenkins, Pte R Davis,
Miss C Sheppard; Seated (from left): Jack Hewitt - Corps Superintendent, G Reason - Div. Officer,
Miss M Mansfield and Div. Superintendent A Francis

St John Ambulance Parade in Dover, 1939

Jack, Area Superintendent in 1978

In 1938 we had a three county St John Ambulance parade in Dover. It was the biggest ever with over 2000 people taking part. Afterwards St James' and St Mary's churches were packed for special services.

After the War I became an Ambulance Officer, then Ambulance Superintendent and later Area Superintendent in charge of 11 Divisions from Dover to Dungeness and from Tenterden to Maidstone. I was made Divisional Officer in 1949 and then Divisional Superintendent in 1958. In 1961 I was made a Serving Brother of the Order of the Hospital of St John of Jerusalem for outstanding service and, in 1978, an Officer of St John. I went to the opening of the new Kent St John HQ and training school at West Malling and was presented to the Duke of Gloucester as the longest serving member in Kent, having done 67 years.

Skeleton service

Sometime in the 1940s I gave a first aid talk to members of TocH at their HQ in Priory Road. Little did I know that I was speaking in a chapel dedicated in 1253 to Saint Edmund who was Archbishop of Canterbury 1234-45. I had borrowed a skeleton from the Royal Victoria Hospital for demonstration purposes. After the meeting there was an accident outside the Town Hall, so I put the skeleton in a shop doorway, sent somebody to get a trolley from the hospital up the road, took the patient to the hospital and then went back for the skeleton only to find a young lad lying by the skeleton in its box. I discovered afterwards that he had opened the box, saw the skeleton and promptly passed out!

I have given many talks on first aid over the years but an unusual one was when I gave a talk and demonstration of resuscitation of cardiac massage to 300 chartered physiotherapists in private practice who were meeting at The University of Kent.

Helping out

On three different occasions I gave up a week's leave from the ambulance service to spend time as a St John worker at camps for the physically handicapped at St Margaret's Bay, at Golden Sands Dymchurch and at Hayling Island. I did some weekends as well. That was very satisfying. I also have fond memories of helping to load sick pilgrims on to the ferries on their way to Lourdes. In 1982 I was privileged to visit Lourdes and was very impressed with the hospitals there.

In 1956 I had a week's sick leave with a septic thumb caused by a rose thorn, so I went to Connaught Barracks to help with Hungarian refugees. Countess

Mountbatten asked me to take charge of a train from Dover to Edinburgh, which only stopped at Canterbury to pick up first aiders and food. Even though we left Dover Priory station at 6.30am, Countess Mountbatten was there to see us off and to say thank you.

Once, in 1956, I was a member of the crew of Dover Lifeboat for one trip! I was going down Maison Dieu Road to see a scout about some badges when the Lifeboat maroon went off. I saw this car going to the Lifeboat Station and I asked for a lift. When we arrived I asked Coxswain Walker whether he needed another crewmember and he did. So I went aboard even though I'm a terrible sailor, but I was fine. We spent four hours in the Channel rescuing four doctors from Hammersmith.

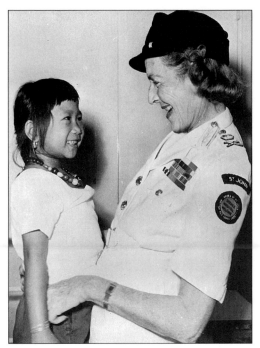

Countess Mountbatten, Superintendent-in-Chief, shortly before her death

Racing at Lydden

One day in 1960 the St John attended a stock car event at Lydden. There was a stunt where a car roared up a ramp to leap over several other cars, but it caught the top of one of them. The stunt car ploughed into the crowd standing 10 deep. Bodies were hurled into the air and people were screaming. The driver fractured his skull and 20 other people were injured. I called for any doctors in the crowd to assist with the injured, but there was only one, Doctor Garrard. He had taken his son there. He was very well organised and saw the injured one after the other. A three years old boy had his leg amputated and his grandfather was killed. I was commended for that and for four other incidents during my service from 1946 until 1975. St John members, including myself, attended the Lydden race meetings from 1947 until the track closed in 1985. My free pass to Lydden isn't much good now!

Lydden Race Track, 1950 with George Hubbard, Divisional Officer, Canterbury

Thumbing a lift from Steven Spielberg

On another occasion I had managed to get a week's leave to provide first aid when they were filming *Battle of Britain* behind Shakespeare Cliff in Dover. A helicopter had to take up a model Dornier aircraft and then drop it to be filmed as part of the trick photography, but the stunt pilot wouldn't go up. The weather was really atrocious. So the director told another pilot to take the helicopter to Ashford Airport at Lympne, but he didn't know where it was. So I said that I knew where it was and I had a map so could I go with him. Off we went. I was really scared. The helicopter just shot up into the air and I thought we were going over Shakespeare Cliff and into the sea. However, once we were airborne it was all right. I found the tower of Hougham Church and then the Blue House at Newingreen. I told him to go right, but he said that he could see the airport. I replied that I wanted to fly over the Brabourne Estate first! 'You'll get me shot,' he said. We landed at Lympne and then I had to find my own way back to Dover. I flagged a car down and said, 'Greetings, gentlemen, where are you going?' 'We're going to Dover to play cricket at The Danes.' 'Have you got room for me?' I asked. I got in, showed them how to get to The Danes but they wanted to eat somewhere first so I directed them to the Market Square. As we parted company I said to them, 'Did you think I was a policeman?' 'Yes, they replied.' 'Well, I'm an ambulance man!' I still had to get back to Shakespeare Cliff, but then I saw Steven Spielberg, who was directing the film, getting into his car. I went across and said, 'Ah, sir, I'm helping up at Shakespeare Cliff with your filming. Could you give me a lift back?' He did. The whole return journey had taken just five minutes over the hour to complete. That wasn't bad going, was it?

Lord and Lady Guilford

In 1962 as I was sitting outside Dover Library on St George's Day waiting for the Zeebrugge memorial service to start. One of our ambulance drivers walked by and so I waved my hand and shouted, 'Greetings, Ron.' He waved back and so did a lady. I saw that it was Lady Guilford. She went to a nearby shop and bought two red roses, then came up to me. I stood up and said, 'Lady Guilford, don't think that I was waving or calling to you. I was calling to a friend of mine. She replied, 'I **am** your friend!' She was a lovely lady who remained a good friend. She was president of the Dover Nursing Division and later became County President. Sadly, she died in 1992.

In 1971 I went out to see Lord Guilford by appointment about a St John Ambulance Brigade project – he

Lady Guilford

61

Earl of Guilford inspecting cadets in the 1960s

was our president. I always made an appointment through his secretary. When I arrived Lord Guilford invited me to see their newborn baby, Piers. They lived in an old Georgian farmhouse with very rickety stairs and up we went. We crept into the baby's room speaking quietly, but the Earl said something that made me laugh and I can't laugh quietly. It woke the baby and up came Lady Guilford and said, 'You're the only one that could do this to me, Mr Hewitt. It took me such a long time to get him off to sleep!' She was quite nice about it – a lovely person. Neither of them ever called me Jack.

Some years later, I asked the Earl whether I should call the child Lord North. 'Use his Christian name, Piers,' said the Earl; however, the Earl called him 'P'nut' at home and apparently friends and family still call him 'P'nut,' even though he is now the Earl!

A toast

When I was invited to the wedding of a St John Ambulance Nursing Officer's daughter, a Miss Pinnock, for some unavoidable reason I was 90 minutes late arriving. I apologised, got on to the stage and said that I would like to toast the bride and groom:

Here's to the good of your blood,
Here's to the good of your health,
The good of your health
Depends upon the good of your blood,
So here's wishing you bloody good health!

People were a bit shocked because I don't swear, but I got that toast from a Scot and thought it appropriate!

Benedictine soup

One Christmas I was in Ealing and on Boxing Day I thought I would have a look at Ealing Benedictine Monastery, but when I tried to get in I was told that they were too busy. I persisted and a monk showed me round. On the way out I heard laughter coming from behind an old door. Being me, I opened it and looked inside. It was the Prior and some of the monks. I was invited to join them at their meal and was presented with a large bowl of soup. I apologised and said that I didn't like soup. They laughed because it was tea! The Prior was sitting in a chair bearing the cross of St John, which had been given to them by the Roman Order of St John. I told them that the Order of St John was the oldest order in the world. This was news to them for they thought the Benedictines were the oldest, but the Benedictines are not really an order, apparently, since each group is more or less independent.

Queen Mother becomes Lord Warden

In 1979 the Queen Mother was installed as Lord Warden of the Cinque Ports. Keith Tutthill was the local St John Superintendent but he was tied up with his business and asked me to organise the first aid arrangements. We had to have 11 first aid posts along the route: at Dover College, the Library, Boots the Chemists (which was used when one of the mounted guards was thrown and had to be treated), St Mary's Church, Granada Cinema and several others. We had to have reinforcements to man them all. Ian Gill, Register of the Cinque Ports, who was in charge of the procession arrangements, said that as I had done so much work I should attend the official dinner for the Queen Mother in the Maison Dieu, not in the main hall with all the dignitaries but up in the gallery. There were eight of us up there and we were waited upon with the same menu as the rest. The Master of the Horse, all dressed up in ceremonial uniform, was one of the eight with a couple of detectives. He kept asking me questions about the first aid arrangements and I wondered whether he was really interested or just being polite. He told me that the Queen Mother would ask him all about the arrangements later and would expect him to know.

Before the event I had had to go to a planning meeting at Constable's Tower, the residence of the Brigadier, the Deputy Constable of Dover Castle. I arrived early and was met by the Brigadier's wife. I told her what a wonderful place her home was and she invited me to look round. It really was, and still probably is, a fabulous historic place.

Centenary of St John 1987

The first meeting of the Dover Division was at the Co-operative Hall, Biggin Street on 12th October 1897; the first Superintendent was Dr. Ian Howden and the first president was Mr. E.P. Barlow of Buckland Paper Mill. After some years the meeting place was changed to the outpatients' department of the Royal Victoria Hospital where we stayed until 1933. Then we moved again into the former Christ Church School in Military Road. The opening was a magnificent

Winning team, Dover Division Challenge Cup, 1900

Dover Division, 1906

affair with a St John Ambulance band leading a march through the town to the new headquarters. Unfortunately, nobody had a key and somebody had to go up a ladder and break in! It was bombed during the War. Pre-War the division was strong in numbers, keen and very competitive. The division's strength was at its

Furley Litter, 1906

Dover Division, 1911

Dover Division's first motor ambulance, 1924

Dover Nursing Division including Jack's mother, 1928

New ambulance, 1930

Dover Division with the Toland doctors, 1934

Marching to the opening of Military Hill HQ in 1933

Opening of the Military Hill HQ in 1933

Cadets, 1939

Opening of the rebuilt HQ in 1954

greatest in 1942 when it was 70. After the War, we worked hard to reorganise and to raise funds to rebuild our HQ. What a wonderful day it was when we finally entered our new home on Military Hill in 1954.

In 1987 an exhibition was held in the Town Hall to mark the centenary of the St John Ambulance Brigade and the 90th anniversary of the Dover Division. A commemorative service was held at St Mary's Church where a window marking the event was dedicated by Revd. Alan Simper. The window, designed by Lesley Gasking of Dover, depicts the Cross of St John and was donated by Mr Lawrence in memory of his wife who was a Dame of the Order of St John.

Dover Division, 1963 with Earl of Guilford, Dover President

Ready for a training exercise on board a ferry in dock, 1963

75th Anniversary Dinner of the Dover Division in 1972, held at the Dover Stage.
From the right: the Earl of Guilford, the Mayor of Dover Kathleen Goodfellow and Jack

Above and below: Training exercises

Jack with reconstruction of Bleriot plane, 1985

Celebrating the Centenary, 1987

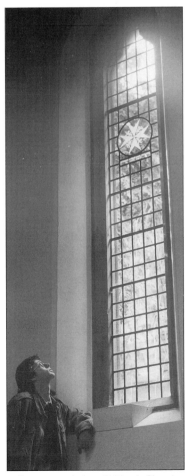

Centenary window, St Mary's Church

"... no dear, it's the Dover Division that's 100 years old ... not Mr Hewitt!" (Centenary cartoon - Dover Express)

Badgers

The Dover St John Ambulance Castle Badger Set was formed in 1987 for children aged six to ten. At its official launch a play entitled *The Badger's Tale* was presented and was so good that they were asked to perform again at Leeds Castle before the Duke of Gloucester, the Grand Prior. St John badgers learn about first aid, safety and health. The Dover Set call me Grandad Badger and their Special Friend.

The first Dover Badgers, 1987

The world's first super badgers being presented to the Queen Mother
(from left Chris Seath (leader), Tina Hall, Veronica Tutthill, Martin Goldsack and Hazel Turner)

In 1988 Veronica Tutthill, Tina Hall, Hazel Turner and Martin Goldsack became the first 'super badgers of the world,' having worked and obtained ten badges in one year. They were presented to the Queen Mother outside the Town Hall and she commented how smart, happy and disciplined they were and a credit to those who instructed them.

The Royals

On 27 February 1996 I was awarded the MBE. I thought it was for community work generally in Dover because the Dover Rotary had given me a community service certificate for that in the previous year, but when the Queen presented me with the MBE, she told me that it was for my St John work in Dover. The Queen was so nice. You aren't supposed to speak to her, only reply, but I said, 'You won't believe this your majesty, but I've been in the Brigade for 65 years.' It was a marvellous day.

I had been to a royal garden party when I was 75 in 1987. In the garden I asked a Beefeater if I could stand beside him. He said that I couldn't, but I could stand behind him and then nobody would stand in front of me. There I stayed and watched the royal party come out. When I was walking round I went to the other two St John people there and was approached by a gentleman who said, 'I notice that you are in the St John and have given long service,' – he could tell that from my medals – 'would you like to have a word with the Grand Prior, the Duke of Gloucester and the Duchess?' Of course, I agreed. The Duke asked me several questions and I didn't let on that on the previous Sunday he had presented me with my retirement certificate at Leeds Castle. Then I said, 'This is certainly a better day than it

Jack in 1996

was on Sunday.' He replied, 'What happened on Sunday?' 'Well, you should know because you got wet through at Leeds Castle.' 'Oh yes, I remember,' said he, 'I presented you with something.' So I told him what it was and then he moved on.

I saw the Duke of Edinburgh and saluted and then saw the Queen and Queen Mother. I noticed something else was happening, the Prince and Princess of Wales were coming along. So I waited and the Prince stopped and spoke to me. 'You've done a lot of service in St John,' he said. 'Yes sir, 57 years,' I replied. 'Why didn't you go on for 60 years,' he wanted to know. So I told him that the

Receiving the MBE from the Queen in 1996

powers that be wouldn't let me, but I would like to have done. 'I'll have a word with the Duke of Gloucester who is Grand Prior of the Order.' But I told him that that wouldn't do any good because we are governed by rules and regulations. 'So am I,' he said! 'Anyway,' I replied, 'I was presented with my retirement certificate by the Duke last Sunday!' We both laughed about it and Princess Di heard us and came over. 'What a laugh,' she said. Prince Charles introduced me to her, told her my story and then she had a good laugh, too. She was lovely. Then I went for some tea but they were clearing away. I had been so interested in what was going on that I hadn't bothered with food. I asked if they could bring something back out for me and they did. I was the last one to leave the tent! It was a good day. I had spoken to four of the eight royals.

Struggling

In October 2001 we held a dedication service for a new ambulance for St John in Dover. In my time I have helped to raise money for five ambulances. It was raining but the photographer was anxious to take a photograph with everybody by the ambulance before the service started. We were all sitting in church, but had

With the Duke of Gloucester, Grand Prior, in 1987

to get up and go outside. I sat tight and people asked me why I wasn't going out. 'I'm not so foolish as everybody else,' I said. 'I'll wait until they are all lined up and ready and then I'll go! Those that go first will get wettest' The brigade in Dover is struggling now with low numbers. There is so much competition for people's time, but there is so much demand for our services. The people still left do an enormous amount of work. Under our new president, Mr Richard Sturt, we are looking for a big improvement in numbers.

Another new ambulance, 1962

Chapter 6

HISTORY OF THE ORDER OF ST JOHN

Most people have seen uniformed members of the St John Ambulance Brigade at public events ready to deal with any accidents and to administer first aid, but few are aware of the centuries of history that lie behind the uniform. In the Middle Ages Christendom was fighting for its life against the expansion of Islam and the Knights of St John were in there fighting. Christendom won that struggle eventually and the Order still flourishes but these days fights suffering and disease.

How did it all start?

A hostel for pilgrims to the Holy Places in Jerusalem was set up by 600AD and continued after the Holy Land was overrun by Moslems. This peaceful co-existence lasted until 1000AD when the Moslem ruler started persecuting Christians and destroyed all their buildings. Later, merchants from Amalfi, a town in Italy that was an independent republic, were allowed to build a church and new hospital for pilgrims. An eight-pointed white cross on a black background was the badge of the Amalfi Republic and was adopted by the monks of the new hospital. It is still the emblem of the Order today. However, persecution continued and the Pope declared a holy war – the Crusades. Jerusalem was captured in 1099 and the hospital was able to care for the wounded and was rewarded by many endowments of land and buildings by Crusaders.

Amalfi Republic's coat of arms

In 1113 a new Order of Hospitallers was founded at the hospital with St John as its patron saint, recognised and protected by the Pope with the privilege of electing their own leader, called Master (later Grand Master). Moslem brigands were molesting pilgrims in the Holy Land and some French knights took it upon themselves to protect them. Others joined and formed a military order with the use of a palace next to the Temple of Solomon and so became known as the Order of Templars. Some of the Hospitallers wanted to help and formed a body of military brothers whilst retaining their duties of maintaining the hospital, nursing the sick and helping the poor. Both Hospitallers and Templars grew in number and wealth, building and garrisoning many castles to guard the borders of the Holy Land and the pilgrim routes.

One hundred years of war began in 1187 when Saladin invaded Palestine and in 1291 the Christian kingdom of Jerusalem finally fell. The Knights decided to continue their charitable work and vowed to maintain an HQ near Palestine in the hope of reconquering the Holy Land. For the next 500 years the Order was an island power in the Mediterranean – in Cyprus for 19 years, Rhodes for more than 200 years and then nearly 300 years in Malta. The banner of St John became the terror of pirates and marauders.

End of the Knights Templars

Templar numbers dwindled with many returning home to their estates and in 1312 the Order of the Temple was dissolved by the Pope and all its property was transferred to the Order of St John. However, in England Edward II claimed all their lands for the Crown until persuaded to hand them over by the Pope! Properties and estates in each country in Europe were controlled by Priors or Grand Priors with one third of the income going to the HQ in the Mediterranean. These priors were members of the international governing body called the Chapter-General, which chose the Grand Master.

The move to Malta

After the Order had been driven from Rhodes in 1522 by the Turks, Emperor Charles V of Austria, in 1530, granted it Malta, which was then a bleak island with 12,000 people. Following a bloody siege of Malta by the Turks in 1565, which was repulsed, and the subsequent defeat of the Turkish fleet, Valetta was built with a new palace for the Grand Master and a great new church and hospital with a single ward 150 yards long by 12 yards wide accommodating 400 patients. So wealthy was the hospital that patients were served food on silver dishes. The NHS will never be as good as that! For the next 250 years the Order served the sick and protected trade in the Mediterranean but by the 18th century it had outlived its purpose. Wealth and idleness set in.

In 1789 as a consequence of the French Revolution all the properties of the Order in France were confiscated and in 1798 Napoleon seized Malta. The Knights scattered, eventually settling in Rome. The Sovereign Order of Malta, which is Roman Catholic, still has its HQ in Rome and the Association of Knights of Malta exists in various countries including Great Britain.

The Order in Great Britain

So what about the history of the Order in Great Britain? In the 12th century the Hospitallers were given land in Clerkenwell, London, where a great priory was built whose gatehouse is still the headquarters of the Order in Great Britain. Henry II gave an estate at Buckland in Somerset as a nunnery for the sisters of the Order. However, in 1540, Henry VIII dissolved the Order, the Crown took all the property and three Knights were executed for treason. Catholic Queen Mary reinstated the Order and restored most of its estates but her sister, Queen Elizabeth, promptly confiscated them again when she came to the throne but never formally dissolved the Order, which then lay dormant for three hundred years. It was kept alive, in name at least, in Malta with the appointment of Grand Priors of England who never came here.

In 1831 the Order was revived in England with protestants admitted, but the Sovereign Order in Rome refused to recognise this version of it and, in 1858, the Order in England became an independent national body but retaining the same traditions and ideals, serving the same cause and wearing the same eight-pointed star. Interest in ambulance and first aid work grew rapidly after the formation of the British National Society for Aid to Sick and Wounded of War in 1870 with

St John Clerkenwell HQ (exterior)

St John Clerkenwell HQ (interior)

many members of the Order joining and helping at the battle front during the Franco-Prussian War. It was soon realised that such help was needed in peacetime as well as war. A voluntary ambulance service was organised in the mining and pottery areas and in 1877 the St John Ambulance Association was founded, followed by the St John Ambulance Brigade in 1887. With the granting of a royal charter in 1888 Queen Victoria became Patron and Sovereign Head of the Order in England with the Prince of Wales as Grand Prior. Since then the monarch has always been Sovereign Head and the Grand Prior has always been a member of the royal family. The Association and Brigade soon expanded into the British Empire.

The full present name of the Order of St John is 'The Grand Priory in the British Realm of the Most Venerable Order of the Hospital of St John of Jerusalem'. The Order is the parent body with the Grand Prior and the Chapter-General as the governing body, which controls the three foundations of the St John Ambulance Association, the St John Ambulance Brigade and the St John Ophthalmic Hospital Jerusalem, built in 1882. The objectives of the Order can be summarised as: first: the encouragement of all that makes for the moral and spiritual strengthening of mankind – in keeping with the first great principle of the Order embodied in its motto '*Pro Fide*' (For the Faith) and, secondly: the encouragement and promotion of all works of humanity and charity for the relief of persons in sickness, distress, suffering and danger without distinction of race, class or creed – the second great principle, embodied in its motto '*Pro Utilitate Hominum*' (For the Service of Mankind).

The work of the Order

First there is the hospital in Jerusalem, which in modern times dates from 1882 when the Sultan of Turkey granted a site for an eye hospital. It gave free eye treatment for the next 66 years during the Turkish occupation and the British Palestine Mandate. It was soon handling 12,000 cases per annum, being the only hospital in the Middle East specialising in eye diseases. It was blown up during World War I but rebuilt immediately after the War in 1918. In 1948 it was severely damaged in the Arab-Israeli fighting and then found itself on the Israeli side of the Arab-Israeli armistice line. Arabs were no longer allowed access to the hospital and its buildings were abandoned but the work carried on in two old houses in Arab territory. In 1960 a new hospital was built in Arab Jerusalem. Fortunately, it was unaffected by the 1967 War except that it found itself in Israeli territory again! I visited it during my trip to the Holy Land in 1962. I took Dover's Brigade flag with me and flew it from the top of the building. It is one of the most up to date eye hospitals in the world with a training school for nurses and a research unit, supported entirely by fund raising and donations.

The St John Ambulance Association was founded with the aims of instructing people in giving first aid, nursing, hygiene and allied subjects; and promoting relief of the suffering and sick. Its work continues to this day throughout the world. The St John Ambulance Brigade aims to provide a properly trained body of people to give first aid wherever required and to provide medical reserves for war and national emergencies. These two arms of the Order were combined in 1968. Cadet divisions were formed in 1922 where people could gain first aid and

Ophthalmic Hospital, Jerusalem

home nursing qualifications as well as proficiency certificates in a wide range of subjects ranging from sailing to cookery. Valuable work was done at home and overseas during the Boer War, World War I and World War II with hospitals, stores depots, ambulances, hospital trains and in providing comforts for POWs. Before the National Health Service it was responsible for providing most of the ambulance services in the UK and still provides that service in Guernsey and Western Australia.

Some time after the Order was revived in England in 1831, it regained its old property in Clerkenwell, which had been in private hands since the Dissolution. Virtually all the original buildings of the old priory have gone, the church has been destroyed and rebuilt several times, but the original crypt still survives as does the gatehouse which is now the headquarters of the Order. Dick Whittington was educated there and when he became Lord Mayor was made a Knight of the Order as were Lord Baden-Powell, Nurse Cavell and Florence Nightingale.

St John Commandery

In 1988 I gave a talk at the St John Commandery to the Dover History Society about the Commandery established by the Order of St John in the 12th century at Swingfield. The large stone building with its lancet windows that you see today was the chapel and is all that remains. It was built between 1145 and 1150 and was founded by the Sisters of the Order who, in their red habits, went about their charitable work in the area for 35 years before moving to Buckland in Somerset in 1180. The Swingfield Commandery was then taken over by the Brothers of the Order until the dissolution of the monasteries by Henry VIII when it became Crown property and was turned into a farmhouse. A large chimney was built

St John Commandery as a farmhouse in 1806

through the roof and the whole chapel was floored over with a storage cellar below. It was used as part of the St John Farm buildings until about 1976 when it was acquired and restored by the Department of the Environment. It is now administered by English Heritage and is open to the public at weekends during the summer. Among its features are a consecration eight-pointed cross, a gallery and an aumbry for keeping vessels as well as two piscinas for washing vessels and

hands. The well preserved lancet windows on the south side are original. In the late 14th century the original steeply pitched roof was replaced by the present splendid crown post roof. Where the shield of the Order was once displayed can still be seen on the outside walls of the porch.

The income of Swingfield came from land rents, a windmill, a dovecote and contributions from the churches of St Peter's, Swingfield, and St Andrew's at Tilmanstone – two churches appropriated to the Order by Archbishop Langton in 1216. This is why the north chancel window of Tilmanstone Church includes the arms of the Order. On the right side of the church's porch is a Maltese Cross cut in the stone. This may be a Consecration Cross or may also signify the patronage of the Knights.

St John Commandery before 1977 restoration

St John Commandery after restoration

We know that in 1338 the Commander of Swingfield was Sir Roger Basset and with him lived a sergeant, bailiffs, stewards, three chaplains, cooks, bakers, chambermen, boys to wait on the Commander, other officials as well as a Serving Brother and a Corrody holder who was a person entitled to accommodation and sustenance at the house as a result of his gifts to the Order.

In 1540, at the Dissolution, the extensive Commandery lands were leased to a Mr Thorgood and T. Horseley; but in 1551 Henry Palmer of Wingham was granted the house and site, which remained in the family until 1770. The site included many buildings to the northwest of the present chapel. By 1806 most of the buildings had fallen down or been demolished, often for their stone to be used in other buildings. How lucky we are that the chapel survived.

It is still a magnificent building. This large, gaunt, stone structure standing near the road from Dover to Canterbury is there for all to visit and to feel a part of the history of the Order, which was once a part of everyday life in England.

Chapter 7

TRAVELS AND ADVENTURES

I have always liked travelling and new experiences. I suppose my first real adventure was my first flight at the age of 16, which was quite something in those days. There used to be ten minute joy rides at the top of Folkestone Hill. I went and looked around the aeroplane and saw it go up and down. One day I saw the pilot going into a house in Pencester Road where he was lodging. So I knocked at the door and spoke to him and made him a proposition, 'I deliver bread and if you give me some advertising leaflets I'll hand them out to customers who I think may be interested and in return I would like one of your flights.' 'You're on,' he replied. After delivering them I went to Folkestone Hill one Sunday afternoon and saw the pilot and he agreed to take me up with his fiancee. It was a three-seater with me in the back. We flew to Calais and back but I stood up to get a better view of the ships and the force of the wind made my nose bleed!

My first foreign trip

When I was 18 and wanted a holiday Father said I couldn't be spared; my brothers, however, weren't interested, but offered to do my work while I went off on my own for five days. It was too late to get a passport of any sort so I took the ferry and train with just my birth certificate and went to Belgium. In Brussels I found this cheap air trip to Antwerp with Sabena. I was held up there because I didn't have a passport. Fortunately, a Customs officer who was also a scoutmaster came to my rescue. I went on to Ypres and by then I was running out of money, but I met a Belgian scout and said I was looking for somewhere to sleep. There

Jack's first flight in 1928, aged 16

was no room in his house but he offered me his father's barn loft. His parents had a big do on celebrating their Silver Wedding and I joined in, then slept in the loft on some hay. Next day I went round the First World War trenches before coming home.

In 1938 I went to Paris with my brother and four other men including Bill Hopper, who later married Kath Sneller of the Dover haulage family. It was a cheap rail trip starting from London but we arranged to get on at Dover and had a first class cabin on the ferry. We left Dover Saturday evening and got back Monday morning after doing a lot of sightseeing. In Paris we hired a taxi driven by a Russian who took us to a Russian restaurant. It is amazing how many people from Dover I met on my foreign travels. Even on this trip I recognised somebody when we were up the Eiffel Tower. It was the son of Mr Walker, the owner of the Grand Hotel. He took us to a bar and bought drinks for all six of us.

Scotland

After the War in 1946 I went hitchhiking with my friend, Arthur Bailey, to Fort William in Scotland. Arthur was a Dover St John Ambulanceman. We climbed Ben Nevis and stayed in Loch Lomond youth hostel; in those days you had to take your own food. We didn't know that but the other people gave us a little of theirs and we managed. A Scotsman got annoyed when I asked for sugar on my porridge instead of salt. On the way to climb Ben Nevis we spotted a house and went to see if we could get some food there on the way back. We got to the front door after being chased by a goose that was acting as a guard dog. The lady warned us that the mountain had claimed many lives and we shouldn't try it, but if we did and we came back, then she could feed us. A group of climbers thought we were chancing it without ropes, but we made it and it was very satisfying even though it snowed. We rested for a while before returning and a curate joined us who had climbed on his own. We made our way back to the little cottage and had a lovely mixed grill miles from anywhere. After leaving the cottage and having climbed Ben Nevis without a problem, we crossed a little stream, stepping from stone to stone, and my ankle turned over. We got back to Dover having hitched both ways. That was the only hitchhiking I ever did.

In 1949 I went to Scotland again, spending two weeks with my friend Scottie – William Duncan – and his parents. I had met him in the RAF in India when he was very ill and I used to sit by his bed. I like to think I willed him to live. He recovered and we decided that after the War we would spend a holiday together. When I got out of the train I asked a policeman where Coaltown was and he said there was no such place. I showed it to him on the map. I was right, but it's pronounced Coolton up there. I got there eventually and waited for him to come home from work. He was a butcher.

My first real foreign holiday was also with Scottie when we toured Norway in 1952.

Malta 1956

A holiday in Holland in 1955 was followed in 1956 with a trip to Malta by train via France and Italy and then by plane to Malta. I went to gen up on the Order of St John and met the St John Assistant Commissioner for the West Riding and his wife staying at a hotel but the Commissioner for the island, Colonel Abela, said that we could be fixed up in the St John headquarters. He and his wife were very kind with their hospitality and showing us around. I found Malta fascinating and went back five times.

Locked in and shut out

Then came another holiday in Holland, two in Austria and two in France. The first

Malta 1956

French holiday was in 1959 with my friend Bernard Wood. We went to Brittany. When looking round Mont St Michel something took my attention and I got locked in for an hour while the rest of the party and the guide went on down leaving me behind. On that holiday there was a ceremony where the Cardinal was blessing all the cars – something to do with Saint Christopher. I was watching from a raised bank and called out, 'Will you bless me?' and he did. Bernard Wood was a rent collector and ran the physically handicapped scouts attached to the 8th Dover, which was led by Gussy Bushell who became mayor of Dover.

I went to France again in 1960 with my friends Roger Palmer and Ken Greenland. We couldn't get in to the casino at Monte Carlo because we didn't have our passports on us. So we walked about three miles back to St Aygulf to get them. I bought one counter in the casino just to prove that I'd been there!

Canada 1960

When I was in Canada in 1960 there was a big hotel in Quebec, called Château Frontenac, built at the same time as the railway. It was enormous and, so that I knew from the outside which room was mine, I stuck a piece of brown paper on my window. Outside I looked up and saw a St John cross underneath my window. Nobody knew why. Nobody at Ottawa HQ knew but when I got to Vancouver I found out that the French Knights of St John had had a big house, called Chateau St Louis, on the site of the hotel. When the hotel was built, the cross was found buried in the ground and was incorporated in the new building. It just happened to be under my window, which was appropriate, wasn't it?

When I reached Ottawa I arrived late at the hotel and asked a lady, whom I thought worked there, for some information, but she was a guest and we chatted until midnight talking about the history of St John. She gave me a lapel badge of a Canadian maple leaf with the St John cross in the centre, which I still wear. She also asked if I would like to go to the St John HQ in Ottawa and she arranged it for me. This Miss Rogers was the Commissioner for St Edward Island and had come to Ottawa to receive some recognition for her work.

I had to visit Niagara Falls, of course, but also wanted to say that I had been to America. So, early one morning I walked across the bridge between

Canada and the U.S., went through immigration controls and had my passport stamped, went outside to look round but nowhere was open not even for a cup of tea, so after a few minutes I went back. The officials were surprised to see me so soon and thought me nuts to have taken so much trouble to get my passport stamped just to stand on American soil.

I went to Canada again in 1989 on a 24 day rail trip from the east to the west coast.

Jerusalem 1962

In 1962 I toured Greece, Jordan and Israel with the Dover firm, Raymond Cook Tours. When we went to Athens in two coach loads we were late for dinner waiting for our luggage to be off-loaded. I went to the tour leader and asked if something could be done to speed things up, but he said not, 'These people take their time.' So I went out and told them to put the luggage back on the coaches and we would sort it out after dinner.

On the Golan Heights the coach broke down and the driver wanted to continue on an old worn tyre, but I said no, we would wait for another coach. Mr Hawkins of the iron foundry, who was on the tour, suggested we went for a walk and we came across a manhole cover from Dover Engineering Works! Our coach stopped on the road to Jericho and I read the parable of the Good

Lynn Canyon Park, North Vancouver, 1989
This suspension bridge, above Lynn Creek, is a section of the Baden-Powell Trail

Samaritan from the Bible. The Hawkins and the Proudlers – Mr Proudler was a dentist in Dover – invited me to join them at a rotary do in Jerusalem, but I didn't want to impose on them and refused. They met with an accident and had to go to hospital. We were in Jerusalem on the day that Eichmann, the German Nazi, was hung in Jerusalem. I've never seen crowds like it. Our bus had to inch its way through with an escort and he was hung half an hour after we left.

We spent Christmas week in the Holy Land. I attended Midnight Mass in Bethlehem and spent much of the week locating sites and ruins dating back to the

Crusader times including the site of the first Order hospital built in 1203. I and a few other members of the group also visited today's St John Ophthalmic Hospital, one of the finest and busiest ophthalmic hospitals in the world. Treatment is free for the poor and very young. I flew our Dover St John flag from its roof, even though the matron said she would be shot if I did. In the evening I decided to go for a walk around the bazaar and was approached by a man who said he was the watchman. He said that it wasn't safe to walk around at night on my own. I told him that with the badge of St John I was wearing and the respect that the hospital had locally, nobody would touch me. Even so, he followed me around until I returned to the hotel. I invited him in for a coffee and as he left I heard him mutter, 'What an extraordinary man!' At the hospital I noticed that Douglas Fairbanks Junior had signed the visitors' book. He is a Knight of the Order. Some years later I went to the annual St John service in London and sat behind him. I tapped him on the shoulder and told him that we had visited the Jerusalem hospital on the same day.

Courier for Raymond Cook Tours

After a holiday in 1963 in Luxemburg with my friend, Bernard Wood, I went to Belgium with a young friend, Gordon Clark, whose father, Alan Clark was a hairdresser and a friend of mine. Gordon, who was about 14 at the time, heard me tell his parents that I was going to Belgium and he asked to come with me. I said that I would love to take him and his parents agreed. We had a wonderful time looking round Brussels and other parts of Belgium. My young friend would occasionally take tea with me on Saturdays after which we would play Bezique for a couple of hours. Apparently Winston Churchill said that Bezique was a fascinating game, in fact the best of all card games. He would invite villagers from Westerham to play at his home, Chartwell, calling them his special Bezique friends.

I booked another Austrian holiday in 1965 with Raymond Cook Tours. Before I went Raymond Cook knocked at my door and asked if I would like to be a tour leader. I was surprised. He wanted me to start that year, but I already had my holiday booked in Austria so I acted as assistant leader on that trip to learn the ropes. The following year I went to Guernsey as Tour Leader and Raymond Cook came with us to keep an eye on me! He was a nice man but a little strange. He always said that the souvenirs of today are the rubbish of tomorrow and always ate his own brown bread. He stayed five days and then pronounced that I was all right to lead on my own. That was the start of 44 Raymond Cook Tours that I led over the next 22 years, both before and after I retired from the County Ambulance Service, until 1987 when I was 77. These tours took me to so many countries including Italy, Switzerland, Majorca, Malta, North Africa, Tenerife, Norway, Jersey, France, Yugoslavia, Denmark and Israel – most of them more than once! I also went on a couple of cruises in the Mediterranean.

It was a wonderful experience being a courier because I met people that I would otherwise never have known: ordinary people, but also an MP, judges, doctors, clergymen and so on. At one time going through the Atlas Mountains just before reaching Fez, a boy was knocked down. I told the driver that I had a first aid kit with me, examined the boy and found that he was all right. When we got back to Heathrow one of my party, a Miss Brown, said, 'Jack, I liked the way you examined that boy.' So I asked her what knowledge she had and she answered, 'I'm the Medical Officer for Manchester.' I never knew who might be in my party and sometimes they didn't use their titles, as with Dr Brown. People came from all over the country on the Raymond Cook tours. Mrs Win Baker from Watford was a regular. Her husband had died and she had been recommended to Raymond Cook for a holiday. I met her on my second trip and she travelled with me every time thereafter except when her daughter had a baby. I had to send her a note as soon as Raymond Cook told me where and when I was going and then she would book to come with me.

Raymond Cook

Raymond Cook was an incredible chap. Before the Second World War he worked in the family business, Clark's Nurseries, which owned several nurseries and a chain of florist's shops employing 300 people in Dover and elsewhere. In his own time, Raymond started arranging holidays for groups of people – parties he called them – including himself, during the 1930s. During the War he lectured on 'Dig for Victory' for a couple of years and then became a lecturer (on 47 topics) to the armed forces. Immediately after the War he started arranging holidays again and decided not to go back to the family firm but to arrange holidays fulltime instead. Seeing people enjoy themselves and helping them do it gave him a lot of satisfaction. First he worked from his home in River and then he built two shops with offices over them at the bottom of Folkestone Road. His travel bureau was in one shop and the other was a Christian bookshop. In its heyday the firm arranged 200 holiday tours a year. Many of his clients were Methodists. Ray was a Methodist himself, a lay preacher, a great supporter of Methodism locally, the National Children's Home and of Dover YMCA. He was also secretary of the Old Pharosians for many years, a leading light in Dover Rotary and founded Dover Round Table. He retired in 1968 aged 70.

Oberammergau

I went to Oberammergau three times. A Dover man on one of the trips wanted to climb a mountain but had never done so. I told him not to but he went all the same on his own. He didn't turn up for dinner; everybody was anxious and some prayed for him. At midnight we raised the alarm and a search party went out. He turned up whilst they were still out looking for him – five men and a jeep. What a foolish thing to do! Coming out of a restaurant in Oberammergau I bumped into Mrs Hedgecock and her daughter from Crabble Hill in Dover. This was yet another of many times that I met people I knew when I was abroad.

Krankies

On one occasion I was asked at the last minute to go to a hotel in Darlington to lead a Christmas party. It was a converted monastery and on Christmas Day a choir came to the hotel and sang from the gallery. On Boxing Day we went to the local pantomime, which was followed by a buffet attended by the Krankies who were starring in the panto. That was quite something.

Holy Land again

I went to the Holy Land three times in all. In 1976 I was going as courier with Raymond Cook Tours, but he rang me up to tell me that he was cancelling the trip because he only had three ladies wanting to go. 'That's all right,' I said, 'If they want to go, I'll pay my way and look after them.' So we went. While we were there two female Israeli soldiers got on our bus and I told them to keep their weapons out of the way – one of the rifles was sticking in my back – they were not at all pleasant! The main thing I remember about that trip was a lovely choir from Canada and another from Norway. Did you know that the maternity hospital in Bethlehem is booked up continuously with mothers from all over the world who want their babies to be born in Bethlehem – at least that was so in 1976; things may be different now!

Guernsey 1966

St John provides the only ambulance service on Guernsey and it's marvellous. I went there for a holiday in 1966 and was taken to the *Flying Christine*, a ship used by St John for rescue work around the island.

Rommel's HQ

We visited Hammamet when we toured North Africa in 1982. As we went past a big house we were told that it was Rommel's wartime headquarters, so I asked to see it but was told it was private. 'Never mind,' I said and led a small group up to the front door, knocked and asked politely if we could look round. The owner agreed and 16 of us looked round this beautiful house complete with swimming pool!

Around the World in 30 days

I did some longer holiday trips of my own during my time with Raymond Cook's firm and afterwards right up to the present time. My first such trip was to Australia in 1967/8. I had to apply for some extra leave without pay. Eventually

Sark 1966, ambulance still in use

it was approved. The main purpose was to visit my sister in Sydney, but I wanted to call on several St John Ambulance stations as well.

My first stop was Singapore. I went into the Cathedral and a young priest showed me round; on the way out I saw a canon who apologised for not having the time to help me. He told me that he was going to the Trafalgar Home, a leper colony. I asked if I could go with him and he agreed. The first thing I did when I got there was to shake hands with some lepers and was then told to scrub up! It was a big colony that had its own Brownie pack. That was quite an experience.

From there I went to Darwin. There had been an outbreak of foot and mouth in England and I had hush puppy shoes on. The airport people insisted that my shoes had to be disinfected. My new shoes that I had with me and had never worn were taken from me and impounded. Later, I wrote to the Australian Government and eventually they paid me for my missing shoes. From Darwin I went on to Alice Springs. I had already written to the Flying Doctor Service there asking permission to fly, but they told me I would have to get permission from the governor. So I wrote to the governor and on my fifth and last day at Alice Springs I got a call from the Flying Doctor Service to join an emergency flight. I was halfway through breakfast but I left everything and went. I was dressed only in my shirt and shorts and took nothing else with me except some money. We took off and the pilot took me down low to see some crocodiles in the water. We flew on and picked up a lady at Tennant Creek, but she was such a big lady weighing 20 stones that they had to leave me behind! I was due to leave Alice Springs the following morning and there I was 400 miles away! I walked over to the driver of

a lorry and asked if he was going to Alice Springs and he said he might possibly be going tomorrow or the day after. That was no good to me so I started walking! While I was walking, a car passed me but didn't stop. Then a dingo, a wild dog, came up to me and I came out in gooseflesh and stood absolutely still. Later I found out that that was the right thing to do. Even now whenever a strange dog passes me, I come out in gooseflesh! Eventually a car pulled up and this chap said, 'I heard that you were on the road. You're a ruddy fool!' He had come from Darwin and had been told that I was on the road. He gave me a lift but he was the worse for wear! I offered to drive but he said, 'No. You have to have the eyes of a lynx on this

Getting friendly with a boa constrictor

90

road.' A quarter of an hour later he hit a kangaroo and broke its legs. He said that we would have to kill it otherwise the vultures would have it but he had left his rifle behind. He told me to kill it as he had given me a lift! I picked up a large stone and then saw the kangaroo's lovely eyes looking at me. I had to hit it a couple of times. That really upset me and I couldn't stop thinking about it for days. After about 200 miles we pulled up at this place where there was a petrol pump and a little old shack. 'This is a hotel,' he said, 'We'll get something to eat here.' We went in. Its walls were whitewashed with a picture of the Queen on one wall and there were two trestle tables plus a small bar. 'This is a peculiar hotel,' I said. 'Don't you make fun of our hotels,' he barked. Anyway, I got back to my motel in Alice Springs and took off for Sydney via Adelaide on 24 December because I was spending Christmas with my sister.

I stayed with her for a week and then found some cousins near Brisbane. I had never seen them before but I recognised one of them because he was the image of my uncle. I was swimming in the sea when I saw Mr Spain get out of the water. He had lived in Heathfield Avenue in Dover and had emigrated but we recognised each other. It's a small world, isn't it? That was a very special day for me because when I was in Sydney I had heard the kookaburra but not seen it, but at my cousin's I saw a kookaburra sitting on the fence. I was also told that a platypus had been seen in the river. To see it would be a once in a lifetime occurrence. So I went down to the river and, blow me down, I saw it! Then, at the end of the garden, I picked up a small boa constrictor and put it round my neck – my cousin nearly went round the bend! Those three things all happened on the same day. I have been to Australia three times and on the last visit there was a shark in the sea at Rockingham. I had never seen one before. Everybody else left the water in a hurry except me. I was fascinated. It just glided past me with my sister screaming, 'Come out, Jack!' It wasn't a very big shark anyway, only about three feet long. 'It won't hurt me,' I said, but it came back, so I got out of the water! Then my sister held a barbecue and invited lots of friends. In Australia all the men get together and all the women get together for some reason. It just happens like that. My sister's friend brought some other friends including a couple who had lived at St Margaret's Bay and were undertakers. I used to camp with him. 'Good God!' he said, 'Fancy meeting you!'

I could actually feel the silence in the outback. It was quite eerie. Another remarkable thing was watching kangaroos boxing. That was really something. There were also great big natural marbles as large as houses one on top of another. Absolutely fantastic they were. I have tried unsuccessfully to find out how they were formed.

I couldn't fly direct to Fiji because of an airline strike but went via Wellington, New Zealand for a day and a night. I went out with the St John there and took a ferry trip just for the ride, got off and went for a meal. Somebody on a bus spotted me, got off and said, 'Jack, what are you doing here?' He was a Dovorian and I hadn't seen him since the War. He took me to his home and I nearly missed the ferry back.

In Fiji I met the Ambulance Superintendent, who was Chinese, but after 10 minutes there was an explosion on a ship so we went off and dealt with this lady who was badly burnt. The Superintendent then invited me to a Chinese wedding the next day. He said that it would be all right because there would be so many people there that I wouldn't be noticed! In fact, people kept asking me who I was. From Fiji I flew to Honolulu for a couple of hours, then via USA back to England.

Down Under 1981

In 1981 I went to Australia again with permission to wear my Brigade uniform and with the dual purpose of seeing my sister and to meet and work with other members of St John Ambulance. My first visit was to Armadale, 14 miles from Perth, where I met Bill Pinkney at the local ambulance station. He had been an ambulance man in Deal before emigrating in 1971. I also visited the Association HQ at Belmont outside Perth and was shown around. It's responsible for the entire ambulance service in Western Australia (there are no NHS ambulances) and is in contact with the hospitals and the Royal Flying Doctor Service.

I spent three days with them. They knew that I was coming because I had written in advance and asked to meet some of the St John members and look around. On arrival I was given a white coat and was ready for action. My first job was to go to Jandakot Airport where a six weeks premature baby had just arrived by air after a 175 miles journey and was suffering from a respiratory condition. Other jobs included two car crashes and two heart attacks. That shift lasted from 10am to 9pm during which I visited 5 different hospitals. I did two more shifts after that.

Flying Doctor Service

A few days later I went to meet the staff of the Flying Doctor Service at Jandakot Airport and they seemed to be just as interested in me as I was in them. In the Control Room I asked if there was any chance of going up as an observer, but they said no. I asked who gave permission and they told me the Chief Pilot,

Visiting the Flying Doctor Service 1968

Captain John Smith. So I went along the corridor and knocked on his door and said, 'Morning sir. I'm just out from England.' 'Come in,' he replied. 'What are you doing here?' 'Well,' I said, 'I was down here the other day when they were dealing with a premature baby and I wondered how it got on.' 'How did you get involved?' 'Well sir, I did three days with the ambulance service as an observer and this baby was fighting for its life and I wondered whether it survived.' It hadn't. 'You must be very keen,' he said. He asked me what I knew about the Flying Doctor Service and I told him that it was started after the First World War by Revd. Flynn. 'You seem to be very interested. Would you like a coffee?' Yes please, sir,' I replied. He chuckled, 'If you call me 'sir' once more, I'll kick your bloody backside!' Over coffee I said that I would do anything to go up with a flying doctor; I didn't let on that I had been flying at Alice Springs back in 1968! 'No problem,' he said 'I'll have you up within the hour.' Within two hours I was in the air as an observer with the Flying Doctor Service going to Geraldton to pick up a lady who had been hit in the eye with a golf ball. When we got back I thanked the Chief Pilot and he said that he hoped to see me again. I ended up doing four flights! This was a dream come true. Having once qualified as an air attendant in England stood me in good stead. I spent three days at Jandakot flying hundreds of miles in Piper and Beechcraft aircraft. Everybody was very kind to me. I did some more normal ambulance duties before going on a 370 miles train journey to the Gold Country. I stayed at Kalgoorlie, went down a gold mine and later panned for gold, bringing back a small sample. I gave a talk to the Kalgoorlie St John Division about the Brigade in England and was then taken to a saloon to rub shoulders with gold diggers.

Anzac Day

I was invited to attend the Anzac Parade in Perth, marching with a small contingent of 25 St John Ambulance people – the rest were on duty. Anzac Day is Australia's big day of the year. It starts with a dawn parade at 6am followed by a march through the city and a service at the State War Memorial. I marched behind the St John Ambulance Commissioner and felt very proud to be part of this worldwide organisation. Although 6,000 people were marching I was easily spotted because my uniform was black, everybody else in St John was in greyish blue. I was recognised by a man who used to work in Dover's Market Square many years before.

Whilst I was visiting the Western Australia Institute of Technology, the *White Cliffs of Dover* was played over the air and an announcer said that I was visiting Australia and would like to hear from any former Dover people. A lady whose husband was Mr Igglesden of Igglesden and Graves, the bakers in Dover, rang me and sent her love to everyone in Dover. I had a wonderful time in Western Australia and was full of admiration for the St John Ambulance Service there.

Humanitarian aid convoys

In April 1991 I went on my first humanitarian aid convoy to Romania. I had to reduce my age by ten years to be accepted, but before I went I said to the chap running it, a policeman from Folkestone, 'I lied about my age but I don't want to go with a lie on my lips so I have to tell you that I'm ten years older than I said.'

'Well, you look pretty fit to me,' he said, so I went as assistant ambulance driver and first aider and I had to supply food for five people. That was my team. Needless to say, at 79 I was the oldest. Everybody else called me 'Securitaty' because I looked after the bags.

It was the largest convoy ever to leave this country, involving 95 vehicles and 303 volunteers, carrying 120 tons of aid. The journey was hard going. At times

Loading for the Romanian convoy

Romanian convoy: journey's end

we travelled all night, sleeping and eating whenever we had the opportunity. We arrived at Bucharest at midnight and visited a neurosurgical hospital the following morning; we were not allowed inside but left some supplies. We went on to Colentina Hospital for infectious diseases where we spent three days. I saw for myself the legacy left behind by Ceaucescu, the Communist dictator. All the children I came into contact with had either hepatitis, aids or meningitis. The scenes we faced were tragic and it was hard to keep the tears back. The worst part of the trip was coming home and leaving the children behind. I felt very proud and privileged to have been allowed to take part.

The second time I went clashed with an invitation to St George's Chapel, Windsor in 1992 to attend the parade of Queen's Scouts in front of the Queen and the Chief Scout following the award of the Silver Acorn to me. So I attended and then flew out to Romania and caught up with the convoy. I spent a week at a children's orphanage, which was very sad, since the children were suffering from aids, hepatitis, meningitis and so on. At the back of the home was a man who spent his time making small coffins because none of the children would reach the age of eight.

Before going on the convoys I had to raise some money. 'No problem,' I said. I've always been good at raising money. I made a board publicising my trip and the need for money and then paraded up and down the town looking for sponsors for a walk to Canterbury. Somebody stopped me and asked how much I wanted, '20 pence to do the walk,' I said. 'That's ridiculous,' he replied. Anyway, in a fortnight I raised £1,143.43p. I did the walk, of course, sponsored by 1500 people and set off at 6 o'clock in the morning accompanied by two nursing cadets, Joanne Culmer and Emma Campbell, Sarah, Teresa and Susan Munn, two senior scouts, Paul McConnell and John Scott and an army cadet, Vaughn Gledhill. It took me four and a half hours. It was the laughter and encouragement of the young people that kept me going and I was mighty pleased to reach Canterbury.

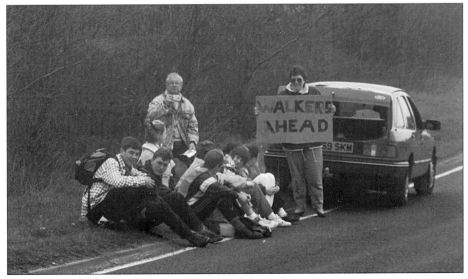

Walking to Canterbury

Alaska 1993

I've been to the North Pole! I actually went there because it was a place in Alaska with that name, south of Fairbanks. It was an extraordinary place with its own school, its own police force and a very big store. There was a big statue of Father Christmas and the whole place was decorated throughout the year. We arrived at Juneau, the capital of Alaska, which can only be reached by sea or air and sits at the bottom of the Mendenhall Glacier. I visited the world famous Red Dog Saloon where I had a certificate signed by three drinking witnesses. I was made an honorary member of the Arctic Brotherhood. I also visited the capital of the Yukon, Whitehorse, went to City Hall and asked to see the Mayor stating that I was bringing greetings from the citizens of Dover. I spent an hour with him after which he gave me his card and a Whitehorse buttonhole badge, which he told me to wear at all times to remind me of this wonderful trip. At Beaver Creek I stayed in a log cabin and was also given a certificate for enduring the 1500 miles along the Alaskan Highway. I panned for gold in Fairbanks and made a find worth about £7 and then travelled north into mountainous country where I saw 12 bears which was very fortunate. Some people never see them on this trip. I also had a 200 miles round trip by light plane and then 40 miles around the 20,203 feet snow capped Mount McKinley. There were 600 glaciers in the area. I think that Mckinley is really a higher mountain than Everest if you ignore sea level and measure from base to summit because Everest is 29002 feet above sea level but only 11,000 feet above its foothills; McKinley is 20,203 feet of which 19,203 feet is above its foothills. The mountain was named after the USA president, William McKinley, in 1896.

Toys for Russia

Toys for Russia

In 1994 I collected 526 cuddly toys, which went to Russia, Romania and war wounded children in Bosnia. Anneka Rice had been to this children's home at Komso and the only things they were short of were toys. So I went to the travel agent and asked whether there was any chance of getting to Russia. There was, so I booked up and then asked for 100 toys in the *Dover Express*. Instead of 100 I received 526! My sitting room was full of teddy bears and what have you. I

96

wrote to Heathrow and told them that I would be bringing 153 cuddly toys with me and asked whether there would be a charge. Apparently it would all depend on how many passengers they had etc. so I took them with me anyway. On the way I had to get people to help me all the time because there were so many. When we arrived at the cruise ship at St Petersburg I had to have help with the toys again. We had coach trips for three days and each day these toys had to be loaded on to the coach in case we passed the hospital they were destined for. I didn't know where it was. The crew of the cruise ship were from Moscow and didn't know anything about this hospital in St Petersburg. Nobody did! As we toured around I looked for it. On the last day I recognised from Anneka's television programme the prison, which was next door to the hospital. 'This is it', I shouted and people on the coach helped me off with the toys. I rang the bell and told them who I was and what I was up to.

Some of the remaining toys went on a convoy to Bosnia and the rest to Romania. I got a letter from a monk in Romania thanking me.

I enjoyed that trip, especially St Petersburg with its 42 islands and 663 bridges, the Bolshoi Ballet and the Russian State Circus – not to mention Red Square in Moscow complete with the Kremlin and Lenin's Mausoleum.

The Northern Expedition 1995

When I was 83 I took a 17 days cruise ship holiday on the *Southern Cross*. We started from Tilbury, crossed to Rotterdam, stopped off at Lerwick in the Shetland Isles and Reykjavik, the capital of Iceland, where I was entertained by the local scout movement, which was formed in 1912. They were very interested

Snowmobile on the Columbia Icefield, Iceland

to learn from me about scouting in England. Then we went on to Spitzbergen. The capital is Longyearbyen. It was quite an experience being 400 miles north of Norway and then, at Magdalena, being only 140 miles from the North Pole. We called at several ports in Norway and missed by one day a bear that attacked the husky dogs for food. It was shot with a dart and taken away by helicopter.

Magdalena Bay, Spitzbergen 1995

Kenya 1996

1996 was the year I received my MBE but I had to cancel my holiday in Kenya, lose my deposit and rebook for a week later because it clashed. I wanted to be in

Baden-Powell's grave at Nyeri, 1996

Kenya on the Chief Scout's birthday but couldn't. I stayed one night in Treetops where Princess Elizabeth was staying in 1952 when she heard that her father had died and she was Queen. I also went on safari. Before I went I gave a talk to St Mary's cubs and told them I was going to Kenya and was going to lay a wreath on Baden-Powell's grave from all the scouts in Dover. After my talk, a little cub came up to me afterwards and said that he would like to give something toward the wreath and took 10 pence out of his pocket and gave it to me. I thought it was a good idea, so when I went visiting the scout troops I invited them to give a few

Commissioner and his family, Nyeri, Kenya, 1996

pence toward the wreath. It raised £140. I gave £30 to the scout troop in Nyeri near where The Chief was buried and gave the rest to the Scout Association. I also took out with me a canister containing the 631 signatures of those who had given money to burn over the grave with the smoke rising as a symbolic prayer of thanksgiving for Baden-Powell's life. I spent many hours on the veranda of the cottage, where he lived from 1938 to 1941, watching the changing scenes over Mount Kenya 40 miles away.

The Himalayas 1997

In 1997 I went to Nepal and the Himalayas. I visited the Scout HQ at Katmandu and went on to Pokhara in a 12 seater plane. Then I went to Chitawan in the jungle for an elephant safari. I lost my hat while I was riding on this elephant but it retrieved it for me with his trunk! I shot wild boar, one horned rhinos and crocodiles – but only with my camera!

Elephant safari, Himalayas, 1997

Pokhara airport, 1997

China 1997

I celebrated my 85th birthday with ancient Chinese warriors. I was on holiday in China visiting one of the world's greatest archaeological treasures: 8,000 life-size, terracotta warriors and horses dating back 2,200 years. I also visited the Great Wall, Tiananmen Square and a panda zoo. It was a fantastic experience with so many wonderful places to see and explore.

Jack with 4 of the 8,000 life-size terracotta warriors; below: Tiananmen Square, China 1997

Tiananmen Square

G. U. M. Department Store, Red Square, Moscow

Russia 1998

My second trip to Russia was in 1998 from Moscow to Rostov – 800 miles by train travelling overnight. At every station on the journey we were only a minute or two early or late and the train was bang on time at our destination; I thought that was terrific. The Moscow Underground was something out of this world with beautiful murals and paintings – no graffiti. One station was all marble. I cruised the River Volga from Moscow to the Caspian Sea. The Volga is the fifteenth longest river in the world. It was 2290 miles long but is now only 1980 since Stalin created a short cut to the sea by building a canal with forced labour that moved 200 million cubic metres of earth. One morning I woke up on the boat with cornfields all around us and there was a ship coming through them, or so it seemed; in fact it was on the river but round a bend. This ship, as big as a cross Channel ferry followed us for miles and miles. I give talks about my trips to Russia.

Ukraine 1999

In the following year I flew to Kiev in the Ukraine and then went by river boat to the Black Sea and saw the Crimean War battle sites. On the spot where Lord Raglan gave the order for the Light Brigade to charge I stood and read the famous poem.

Antarctica 1999/2000

Antarctica was my most recent expedition. I wanted to do something different for the Millennium and saw this advertisement and wrote to the company but received no reply. I wrote again and received a lot of stuff but nothing about an expedition. So I went to Thomas Cook and said that I wanted to do something different for the Millennium. Later, they phoned to tell me that they had got something, a cruise to the Antarctic! There were sixty people and 12 qualified leaders: scientists, explorers, marine biologists and all that. I didn't declare my age but I got my doctor to declare that I was completely fit; although, I wasn't really because I was suffering from gout! I had to state that I could walk four miles over difficult ground, which I would have had difficulty doing, but I thought that was just something to cover themselves. Anyhow, I coped all right.

I flew to Buenos Aires, stayed there a day and went on to Ushuaia, the southernmost town in the world, where we toured the Tierra del Fuego national park in the far south of the Argentine. At Ushuaia we boarded the *Caledonian Star* and headed for the Falklands. As we cruised along we began our fascinating programme of on board lectures about the wild life, flora and fauna that we would see. The Falklands comprise two larger islands and 200 smaller ones. We were welcomed by jackass penguins swimming alongside us. We went ashore on several islands and came across geese, cormorants, steamer ducks, rockhopper penguins and albatrosses. We had an exciting landing through the surf at one island but it was worth it to see the king penguins. The wild life was absolutely wonderful. The rockhopper penguins in New Island fascinated me. I watched them for half an hour. They were collecting small stones to build their nests. One male penguin went off searching for stones, brought them back to his nest and went off again. Meanwhile, two other males then pinched his stones! This went on for two or three trips. Then I saw a colony of albatrosses with 14 feet wingspans. To watch them land and take off was terrific. It was nesting time so we saw eggs and young birds.

After visiting four islands in two days, we ended up in Port Stanley on Christmas Day when there was an RAF fly-past over the ship. They said that it was for us, but it probably wasn't! Then we went south, passing hundreds of icebergs, some larger than the Gateway flats. I couldn't believe how big they were. It was a wonderful experience. Going through the Drake Passage on the ship it was very rough – well, it was rough for me. I woke up and found the ship tilted at an angle but I thought that I must get up, so I did and was thrown across

Communing with the Rockhopper penguins, New Island, Falklands

the cabin hitting my head on the door. I was lucky because a lady two cabins away did the same thing and she fractured her thigh and never saw anything after that. She stayed on board because her insurance didn't provide for a helicopter to take her back and it would have cost thousands. An American doctor elevated her leg for her and there she stayed in her cabin until we got back to Chile. Only once did they have to dig me out of the snow and that was on Elephant Island,

Shackleton's base camp, Point Wild, South Shetland Islands

Aboard *Caledonian Star going south, "... icebergs, some larger than the Gateway flats"*

At Cape Horn

following in Shackleton's footsteps. There we saw huge elephant seals, leopard seals and pintado petrels. We pushed on into the Weddell Sea and spent a wonderful evening cruising through the ice. We actually landed on the Antarctic Peninsula and enjoyed more spectacular scenery. New Year's Eve was the most scenic day of the whole trip as we watched humpback whales and edged our way through the pack ice into Paradise Bay, Graham Land where there were two great 9,000 feet high ice mountains. The weather was perfect. It was about 9pm and the sun was beginning to go down. It set at two minutes to midnight and rose again at twenty past two. Both events were absolutely beautiful.

At Cape Horn we went ashore in small craft and had trouble landing on the rocks. We climbed over one hundred rickety stairs to reach the Chilean weather station, which is home to one family that changes every year. There was a very peculiar iron mon-ument made of two vertical pieces, slightly displaced from each other, that I couldn't make head nor tail of. I then went into this tiny church that only held 12 people, but when I came out and looked at the monument from a different angle I could see that it was the perfect outline of an albatross. It is dedicated to the many sailors who have lost their lives around Cape Horn. Sailors believed that souls of sailors lost at sea returned in the albatrosses that soar over the Southern Ocean. On the path by the monument there was a tablet with this poem on it:

I am the albatross who awaits you
at the end of the world.
I am the soul of ancient mariners
who rounded Cape Horn
from all the seas of the world.
They didn't perish in the furious waves.
Today they fly on my wings for all eternity
in the ultimate embrace of the Antarctic winds.

The trip ended at Punto Arenas, the southernmost city in Chile and then we flew back to Buenos Aires before returning home. It was an expensive trip from 19 December to 6 January, but I had the money and thought I might as well spend it. The 14 days of sailing, covering 3,597 miles was a holiday I will never forget.

Health

I didn't plan any holidays in 2001 because of my health problem. The consultant said to me, 'It's make up your mind time. You've got this cancer growth on the oesophagus. We can open you up and take it out.' However, I can't take general anaesthetic. I had a hernia operation once and when I got back to the ward I was asked how I felt. I said that it was strange that the operation was down below but all I had was a sore throat and I was spitting up blood. The doctor said, 'You haven't had the operation yet!' So I asked him why and he told me that I couldn't take the anaesthetic. The surgeon sat on my bed and said that he didn't know what to do. 'Well, if I can't take a general anaesthetic, I'll have an epidural,' I said. 'Thank you very much, you've solved our problem,' he replied! I imposed one condition, which was that once they opened me up, they let me have a look – and they did! There was a lot of pain, which I could just about stand. So I decided that with this cancer I couldn't take a big operation again without general anaesthetic, especially at my age and with only a 50/50 chance of surviving; I opted for radiotherapy.

Chapter 8

RETIREMENT ACTIVITIES

Jewish Girls' and Lads' Brigade

I retired from the County Ambulance Service when I was 65. Then I received a letter from County asking me if I could find somebody to assist the Jewish Girls' and Lads' Brigade at their Kingsdown camp. As I had retired, I did it myself. I went over at 9am and spent the day with them. After dinner I got ready to leave and they asked why I wasn't staying overnight. I thought I was attending on a daily basis, but they wanted me to camp with them. So I went home for my kit and joined them. After that I camped with them in different places for 20 years until I was 85. At one camp the cast of *Jesus Christ, Superstar* came to entertain us. On another occasion I slept with three rabbis, or perhaps I should say that I shared a tent with three rabbis and we had some very interesting discussions. I was only asked to say grace once in all those years. Obviously, I had to be careful what I said even though they said I was more Jewish than a Jew because I obeyed all their rules. After supper I told them what had happened when I went home after the previous camp. I was feeling a bit deflated after it and thinking 'Oh well, back to normal.' I decided to go out for a Chinese meal. As I waited to be served I thought about all the countries of the world where there were Jews: Russian Jews, German Jews, Austrian Jews, French Jews, American Jews etc. When the waiter came for my order I said, 'Do you have Chinese Jews?' He said that he would ask the boss. When he came back he said, 'Sorry, we've only got orange juice or lemon juice.' He wondered why I burst out laughing. I told that story when I spoke at a rotary do and they wouldn't believe it was true.

At my last camp I was told to be in uniform. Over the loudspeaker came an announcement of a special presentation to me by Dame Simone Prendergast for my 20 summer and 5 winter camps with them. They made me an honorary captain of the JGLB and gave me the necessary 'pips'. I am the only non-Jewish member of the JGLB. There is an amusing sequel to this. I went to see the Brigadier at the Dover Castle and noticed that I had the same 'pips' as he did: three crowns. This is because officers of the Girls' Brigade and Boys' Brigade are commissioned officers and are 'gazetted' on promotion. This happened during Queen Victoria's reign and has never been rescinded.

Volunteer hospital car driver

When I retired I became a voluntary car driver for social services. In 1989 I was doing a volunteer hospital driver duty taking a blind lady and her escort to Sandwich. It was a terrible day, pouring with rain. I had to waste some time before taking the ladies back and decided to buy some fish and chips. By the time I had eaten them the weather had completely changed. So I walked along the riverbank toward Pfizer's and reached a high stile and started to climb over it, thoroughly enjoying the scenery. The next thing I knew I was coming up out of the water! I grabbed the bank but it gave way. I was covered in mud and prayed, 'Please God, don't let me die this way.' I did manage to climb out somehow and walked back to the restaurant by the Barbican Gate and asked for a sweet cup of tea. The owner did not want me to drive but I did and picked up my ladies. I went to Buckland Hospital and saw Doctor Charles and told him that I was quite sore and had swallowed a lot of mud. He didn't give me a stomach washout and I was in great pain during the night but it had passed by the morning. Anyway, a month later Doctor Charles rang me and said that he would like to check me out before I went to Canada following 'my dive into the dyke'. I thought that was very nice of him.

Breewood

I spent 7 years – one day a week – looking after 20 or more children at risk at Breewood playgroup in Deal. The week I retired I was contacted and asked if I could help with the voluntary car service transporting children. I went for three or four weeks and then one of the teachers said to me, 'You're fond of children aren't you, Jack? Would you like to be one of the teachers?' 'Yes, I would love it,' I replied. It was all voluntary. There was a little boy that I took to the toilet and I said, 'I think that you're big enough now to go on your own.' He went in but for some reason I opened the door and noticed that there were lines across his bottom. 'How did you get these marks,' I asked. We telephoned social services and both he and his brother were removed and taken to Buckland Hospital. His father had been out of prison just three or four days and had abused him. On one occasion some expert from social services came and said that all the toys had to be out at the same time rather than a selection to allow freedom of expression. It was absolutely chaotic thereafter. Eventually the place closed down because of the cost.

Plumptre of Goodnestone Park

I still provide first aid cover for organisations like Arthritis Care and the physically handicapped when needed. A few years ago I went out as first aider to Goodnestone with a group of blind people and had a strawberry tea there. Lady

Goodnestone Park

FitzWalter sat down with me and I told her that I was there during the First World War and had to sing to Mr Plumptre. I still remember the song because I went over it so many times. I asked her whether she would like me to sing it to her and she said yes. So I stood up and sang it! Everybody laughed. We had a collection for St John there when the house and garden was opened to raise money. I was collecting but asked to be relieved so that I could have a look around the house. I went in and there were two ladies and a man talking in this room. One said, 'The Queen Mother would have sat there,' but the young man said, 'No, she would have sat here.' The ladies went out of the room and I asked the man who he was. 'I'm William, one of the sons,' he said. Apparently, it's the third oldest baronetcy in the country. The FitzWalters accompanied William the Conqueror to England and 150 years later Robert FitzWalter led the Barons who forced King John to sign Magna Carta. In 1295 his grandson was summoned to Parliament as Baron FitzWalter. The title went into abeyance for 168 years, but 'was carried' by the female line, until Henry FitzWalter Plumptre claimed the title in 1924 followed by his nephew, FitzWalter Brook Plumptre in 1953.

Microlites, gliders and helicopters

I have always looked for new experiences. My niece's husband had just qualified as a microlite pilot and I went along for the ride! The wings of his microlite were like the wings of a glider, very long. When I got to Redhill to help assemble it, I found that the wings just slotted in to place. They didn't look very safe; however, I was assured they were. I went up with the pilot and put my camera on the floor but the pilot told me not to do that. With no spare room at all, I had to lift the camera up using my feet and legs until I could reach it with my hand. It was a

Jack's microlite flight at 80

wonderful experience flying over the M25 to Tunbridge Wells and back.

One day a member of St John suggested that we went gliding. So we went as a group to Waldershare Park. It was the only glider flight I ever had but it was a terrific feeling – just like a bird. Absolutely wonderful! On another occasion I was at Waldershare Park with a friend and his lad. I asked if I could take the boy for a helicopter ride. When we were in the air we saw an accident by the High and Dry public house. So we called for an ambulance from the air. By the time people on the ground called for an ambulance, it had arrived and they didn't know how!

Balloon trip

My 80th birthday celebration landed me in hospital! I decided to celebrate by taking a hot air balloon trip over East Kent. I had never done it before. I climbed aboard at Broome Park for the one hour flight and took with me a St John flag, the Dover Town flag and the Union Jack which were tied to the balloon basket. Soon we were up and away floating towards Romney Marsh. It was absolutely fantastic until the landing. I was told to hold on tight, but I don't think I held on tightly enough! As the balloon landed in a field at St Mary-in-the-Marsh it was caught by a gust of wind and I was thrown out. I remembered to tuck my head in and I think that saved me from any more serious injury. The balloon travelled

another 150 yards before coming to rest. Boys from the village helped me into a jeep but we got lost in the fog on the Marsh and arrived at Canterbury Hospital just after midnight. I suffered cracked ribs, cuts to my face and my glasses were broken. The pilot stayed with me until morning and then brought me

80th Birthday balloon trip

home. He insisted upon having the trip on him! I wasn't put off because I went up again in 2000 with Michael Young from River. It was a beautiful evening and we had a perfect landing that time!

Filming

In 1990 I appeared twice in the ITV series, *Spitfire Summer*. Then, in November 1999 I had a phone call asking me if I would go to Dover Castle to do some filming for Yorkshire Television and had to talk about Dover during the War and how Dovorians reacted. They were doing the same thing in other towns with six children finding out how people had coped during the War. Months afterwards, I received an official letter from the Imperial War Museum telling me that the video would be shown in schools as part of the commemoration of VE Day.

On another occasion I had a phone call from Frankfurt asking me to take part in a film, *War of the Century*. I agreed, but they said they would be bringing a lot of equipment to the house. 'No problem,' I said and cleared plenty of space for it. Then I had another call from them telling me that they had a studio at Hawkinge and it would be easier if I went over there. Once again I said, 'No problem. Just send a car for me!' I asked how they knew of me. Apparently they had contacted Roy Humphreys who had written a book about wartime Dover and asked him for the name of somebody who could talk about the War. That will be a German film – an eight part series – and I will be speaking German! Later it may be shown in England on TV. I did something similar for the Second World War street scene in Dover's White Cliffs Experience.

I had yet another phone call in 2001 asking if I would take part in a film to be shot in Canterbury and London. I agreed. This was on the Friday and they wanted me the next day, but I said that I couldn't possibly go on Saturday as it was the St John flag day. However, the filming was already arranged for the Saturday at the University at Canterbury. To cut a long story short we agreed a compromise: I would do my flag selling and a car would pick me up in Dour Street at noon. The film was called *Ashley* and my name was John Ashley. As a young boy John Ashley had met with a swimming accident and later died in hospital. So there was I in bed in this hospital ward set being shot by cameras from all angles for two hours. I said, 'You may as well tell me what my diagnosis is.' I was told it was cancer of the throat. I never let on that I really did have cancer of the oesophagus. I had arranged to help out at the Town Hall that same evening as an usher at the DODS musical show, *Oklahoma*. Filming finished at five to six and the car whisked me back to Dover five minutes before the show started. I was too late to usher but at least I saw the show.

Money raising

I have raised money for the scouts and St John and other good causes for most of my life and I'm still doing it. Ideas seem to come easily to me and the money appears. Perhaps the simplest was in 1999 when I sat on a bench outside the library with a clipboard in my hand and just kept quiet. When passers-by asked me what I was doing I told them I was trying to raise enough money to pay for the hire of Pencester Gardens for the scouts' fête. I wasn't begging but most people gave something and I raised over £100!

Dressing-up

I enjoy dressing up whether it's acting the fool, fund raising, or for something serious like the 1999 Dover Pageant when I dressed as Sir Thomas Docwra, who was St John Grand Prior of England 1501-27 and Lord High Treasurer to Henry VIII, and, of course, as Father Christmas which I have done many times.

Flying the flag

I'm a great supporter of the Royal Family and especially the Queen Mother. In her centenary year Dover produced a commemorative booklet which sold for £1; sellers received 50p per copy for their organisation and the other 50p went towards Dover's Christmas lights. I sold a lot and was doing so during the Queen Mother's visit to Dover. Jenny Bond, the BBC's reporter on the Royal Family spotted me outside the Town Hall asked me what I was doing. I told her and she kindly autographed a copy for me. I sent her a copy later and received a very nice letter back.

Dover Pageant 1999: Jack as Sir Thomas Docwra, Grand Prior of England 1501/27, also Lord High Treasurer to Henry VIII

One of Jack's many appearances as Father Christmas

112

Raising money selling Dover's souvenir booklet
for Queen Mother's 100th birthday

Celebrating the Queen Mother's 100th birthday

On the Queen Mother's 101st birthday in August 2001, I was on the steps of the Town Hall before 9am and when it opened the Town Hall staff said, 'I know what you've come for!' I asked if I could have the honour of hoisting the Union Jack at the top of the Town Hall tower and they agreed. It wasn't easy climbing that very narrow staircase up to the top and I had to do it twice because I forgot to take my camera the first time! It was quite an experience and I also enjoyed the fantastic views of the town from up there.

Local honours

My many years service to the Scout Movement and to the Order of St John has been recognised in various ways by both organisations and by the Queen in bestowing upon me the MBE. In addition, I was very pleased to be

Raising the Union Jack at Dover Town Hall
for the Queen Mother's 101st birthday

awarded the Community Service Award by the Rotary Club of Dover, in 1995, for exceptional service to the Dover community. More recently, in January 2002, I was made an honorary member of the Dover Town Centre Management Committee, following in the footsteps of Terry Sutton MBE.

90th birthday

I celebrated my 90th birthday on 13 February 2002. People were very kind. Things started the evening before, Shrove Tuesday, when I was invited to a pancake evening at St Paul's Church hall. There was a big cake for me and *Happy Birthday* was sung. My birthday was on Ash Wednesday and in the morning I decided to walk to St Mary's for the morning service. On the way the sole of my shoe started flapping and, by the time I reached church, it had fallen off! I took communion standing up rather than expose my problem when kneeling. Afterwards the Vicar asked whether I had a problem kneeling and I replied, 'I lost my sole coming to church!' He thought that was a good pun.

St Mary's lunch club does not normally meet during school holidays because the meals come from the school, but, as it was my birthday, the ladies who serve normally decided to cook lunch, which was very kind. I was presented with a glass tankard engraved, 'Greetings, Jack 1912-2002 from the Lunch Club.'

I had more surprises when evening came. First a deputation of three from St John knocked at my door with presents of champagne, wine and a hamper of groceries. Then the Scouts' Commissioner arrived to give me a lift to a special meeting called, he said, to discuss how the Queen's Jubilee should be celebrated. I had my suspicions especially when he told me we were going to St Mary's

Jack's 90th Birthday celebrations with scout leaders

Church hall. We never meet there! On arrival friends were leaving St Mary's after the evening Ash Wednesday service. I was spotted and they sang *Happy Birthday, Jack.* Inside the hall were about 50 scout leaders representing virtually every group in the district, lots of refreshments and, of course, a birthday cake and *Happy Birthday* yet again! They presented me with a new scout uniform, which I had to put on. This new uniform has to be worn by all scouts by 2003, so I shall have to transfer all my badges! There were other presents including another hamper – I shall not starve for a while – and a three feet high card to go with the other 76 I received.

That was not all. At the weekend my nephew from Temple Ewell collected me after Sunday morning service to take me out to lunch. When we arrived at Pickwicks there were my relations from Gloucester, Colchester, Cardiff, Liverpool and London as well as Temple Ewell – 19 of them aged four months to sixty years! After lunch we went to my nephew's home for yet more birthday cake and champagne and another present, a new television.

It was a great birthday, but perhaps an even bigger event for me will be on 28 March 2002, Maundy Thursday, when I shall be one of those receiving Maundy money from Her Majesty the Queen at Canterbury Cathedral during her Golden Jubilee year. How privileged I am.

Jack taking it easy with Jessica Metcalfe after performing in a talent competition, August 2001

POSTSCRIPT

Ha! Ha! Ha!

My laugh has got me into trouble many times during my life and is quite distinctive! How did I get it? Well, I wasn't born with it. I acquired it from somebody else! When I was young, one of my sisters was courted by a lad called Billy Shepherd and he had this peculiar laugh. When he called for my sister she was never ready and he always had to wait for half an hour or so. He chatted with my dad and I used to hear him laugh. I learned to copy his laugh so that I could mimic him; however, the day came when I could only laugh like him and I've been landed with it ever since!

Final thoughts

Looking back over the past 90 years, I consider that I have had a very good life. I had good and loving parents and we were a happy family. I have seen many changes, some good and others not to my liking! In days gone by most people did not have much, but seemed happier with their lot.

Scouting to me has been a way of life and my association with St John has been a practical way of demonstrating my Christianity. My 30 years in the County Ambulance Service gave me the opportunity to help people as my paid job and I enjoyed every moment.

As an enthusiastic and impressionable 18 year old, full of the joys of living, I immediately found in the St John Ambulance Brigade a wonderful spirit of fellowship and camaraderie. I acquired a sense of purpose and a realisation that no man is an island. 'Service' was a word writ large by my instructors in those early days. Ever since, I have been grateful to them for turning my thoughts to the sufferings and needs of others.

I have travelled far and wide visiting every continent, walked in the most northerly capital in the world and also the most southerly town, visited the lowest city in the world, Jericho, the lowest sea – the Dead Sea, some 1,312 feet below the Mediterranean – and flown over the highest mountain, Everest. I have been privileged to see so many wonderful things in God's world.

I am a man rich in wonderful memories, which increase in value as the years pass. Having led a full and interesting life, I would like to leave this thought with you: do everything in moderation, be happy, think positive and trust in God.

ILLUSTRATIONS

CHAPTER 7

CHAPTER 8

POSTSCRIPT

ACKNOWLEDGEMENTS

We wish to thank the following for their help in the production of this book:

For providing or giving permission to use certain photographs:

Her Majesty The Queen
John Coveney
Bob Hollingsbee
Dover Express
Dover Library
Dover Mecury
Dover Museum
Dover Society (from the Budge Adams Archive)
Kent Messenger
Oliver O'Connor

For meticulous proofreading and helpful suggestions:

May Jones

For the design of the cover and help generally:

The staff of A R Adams and Sons (Printers) Ltd

Information sources:

Canterbury Cathedral Archives for St Mary's Schools' Archive
A Short History of the Order of St John *by E D Renwick, O.St.J.*
Life in Many Parts *by Raymond Cook*